半棒術
HANBOJUTSU

Short stick fighting techniques of the Ninja and Samurai

この本を感謝のしるしとして、初見良昭宗家に謹呈いたします。
I dedicate this book to my teacher Soke Masaaki Hatsumi that without his teachings I would never have been able to publish it, to all my students for having helped me in the making photos and to my family.

Title | HANBOJUTSU: Short stick fighting techniques of the Ninja and Samurai
Author | Luca Lanaro
ISBN | 978-88-27816-22-6

© All rights reserved to the Author
No part of this book can be reproduced without the
prior consent of the Author.

Youcanprint Self-Publishing
Via Roma, 73 - 73039 Tricase (LE) - Italy
www.youcanprint.it
info@youcanprint.it
Facebook: facebook.com/youcanprint.it
Twitter: twitter.com/youcanprintit

Printed in the month of March 2018

INDEX

Foreword	4
Bujinkan Dojo Budo Taijutsu	5
Soke Masaaki Hatsumi	6
Soke Takamatsu Toshitsugu	7
Hanbojutsu no Kigen (Origins of the Japanese short stick art)	8
Sanshin no Kamae (Posture of the Three Hearts)	10
Kiso (Fundamental)	30
Kihon Happo (Eight basic methods)	52
Nage Kata (Form of throws)	80
Muna Dori Kata (Form of the lapel grab)	89
Tehodoki Kata (Form to free the hand)	94
Ushiro Dori Kata (Form of the grabs from behind)	99
Tsuki Gaeshi Kata (Form against fists)	104
Keri Gaeshi Kata (Form against Kicks)	112
Taihojutsu (Art of capture)	120
Kata To Katachi (Form and Form)	130
Juppo Sessho (The art of negotiating in the 10 directions)	155
Ki Nagashi (Energy flow)	161
Bo Nage (Stick throw)	162
Hanbojutsu Densho (Tradition of short stick art)	163
Shoden no Kata (Form of initial transmission)	164
Chuden no Kata (Form of medium transmission)	173
Okuden no Kata (Form of the deepest transmission)	185
Shikomi-Zue (Concealed blade stick)	187
Goshinjutsu (Self-defense)	198
Keisatsu no Taihojutsu (Police arrest techniques)	202
Ihen no Bo (Deception of the stick)	206
Glossary	207
Bibliography	209
The author	210

Foreword

The short stick or any rod has been in all ages, one of the most practical and easy to find weapon. In Japanese this art is called Hanbojutsu 半棒術 translated literally means "art of the half stick", for whole stick in fact is the Rokushaku Bo 六尺棒 or the "long stick" six feet (about 1.80 m) that was used also in combat and therefore the stick Hanbo is its half which is also called Sanshaku Bo 三尺棒 (about 90 cm), depending on the school or Ryu-Ha 流派 the short stick can be of various lengths from 90 cm to 100 cm, and the diameter varies from 2.4 cm to 3 cm, it can also change in shape like the circular Maru 丸 or octagonal Hakkaku 八角 as used in the Kukishin Ryu school, and can be made of iron or various types of wood such as red or white oak.

With this book you can have a complete view of what the Hanbo art consists of as it is studied inside the Bujinkan Dojo, starting from the basic techniques, from the basic Kata that I organized for better understanding by type of attack, to more advanced Kata and of the levels present in the Kukishin Ryu school, the concealed blade stick called Shikomi-Zue 仕込み杖 used above all by the Ninja, and its applications both in the self-defense and how the short stick can be used by the police. Keep in mind that in Bujinkan Dojo first of all is very important to learn Taijutsu or hand-to-hand combat which gives the basis for the movement of the body that is necessary for the use of weapons, because without a proper basis you can't really progress in the training, the training of details from the basics is essential for the understanding of the dynamics of real combat. However, it is very important that you do not try any of these techniques without the supervision of a Bujinkan teacher! Besides being dangerous, it will not give any result especially without the proper oral transmission Kuden 口伝.

Bujinkan Dojo Budo Taijutsu
武神館道場 武道体術

The Bujinkan Dojo 道場館道場 (Residence of the God of War) is the international organization founded by Soke Masaaki Hatsumi for the study and practice of the nine ancient martial traditions that he had inherited. In the Bujinkan Dojo we study the Budo Taijutsu 武道体術 which literally means "the martial art of the body skill", the word Taijutsu 体術 in Japanese is used to define very ancient martial arts, in the Bujinkan Dojo there is the study of 9 schools and their style of combat with bare hands, with their traditional weapons and the philosophy of each of them.

Among these nine schools there is the study of 3 schools of Ninpo Taijutsu 忍法體術 or more easily known as Ninjutsu 忍術 the art of Ninja 忍者, the one most famous Ninja school is the Togakure Ryu Ninpo Taijutsu 戸隠流忍法体術 of the Togakushi village located near the city of Nagano.

The study of bare-handed combat includes the practice of falls, throws, joint locks, levers and how to strike in vital points, in the study of traditional weapons is practiced the study of all traditional weapons of the Samurai 侍 from Bugei Juhappan 武芸十八般 (the 18 arts of war) that add up to 18 of Ninja training forming the Ninpo Sanjurokkei 忍法三十六計 (the 36 Ninja arts). Some schools have an older classification of Bugei Juhappan such as the School Kukishin Ryu Happo Bikenjutsu 九鬼神流八法秘剣術 where the Happo Biken system is studied 八法秘剣 (Eight methods, Secret sword) which consists of:

1) Taijutsu 体術 Unarmed fighting techniques, Hichojutsu 飛鳥術 jumping techniques, Nawanage 縄投 rope throwing.
2) Koppojutsu 骨法術 percussion techniques, Jutaijutsu 柔体術 grappling techniques.
3) Sojutsu 鎗術 spear techniques, Naginatajustu 薙刀術 halberd techniques.
4) Teijutsu 停術 arrest techniques, Hanbojutsu 半棒術 techniques with short stick.
5) Kobannage 小判投 techniques of launching small objects, Tokenjutsu 投剣術 sword throwing techniques, Shurikenjutsu 手裏剣術 blade throwing techniques.
6) Kajutsu 火術 fire techniques, Suijutsu 水術 water techniques.
7) Chikujo Gunryaku Heiho 築城軍略兵法 Strategy tactics of castle building.
8) Onshinjutsu 隠身術 disguise techniques.
❖ Hikenjutsu 秘剣術 The art of the secret sword includes: Ken 剣 sword, Kodachi 小太刀 short sword, Jutte 十手 weapon of the Japanese police of the Edo period and the Tessen 鉄扇 fan.

Starting from this classification later the Bugei Juhappan system it was developed. The Kukishin Ryu school is famous for its techniques with the long stick Rokushaku Bo 六尺棒 and the short stick Sanshaku Bo 三尺棒.

Dojo Kun 道場訓 (Dojo Rules):
1) To know that patience comes first.
2) To know that the path of Man comes from justice.
3) To renounce avarice, indolence, and obstinacy.
4) To recognize sadness and worry as natural, and to seek the immovable heart.
5) To not stray from the path of loyalty and brotherly love, and to delve always deeper into the heart of martial arts.

Meiji 23 First Day of Spring Toda Shinryuken Masamitsu
Showa 33 A Lucky Day in March Takamatsu Toshitsugu Uou
Passed on through Hatsumi Masaaki Byakuryuu

Soke Masaaki Hatsumi
宗家初見良昭

Ph. Masaaki Hatsumi was born in Japan in Chiba Prefecture on December 2, 1931. He graduated from the Meiji University of Medicine where he also studied the traditional theater, arts, painting and Japanese culture.

He has written several books in Japanese and English from Ninjutsu, Budo (Japanese Martial Arts) to poetry, and has made numerous videos on Ninja traditions. He has also taken part in the making of many films, history documentaries, television programs, as well as a consultant on the fight scenes of famous films such as 007 "He lives only twice", in fact he is famous for having directed the fighting scenes for the Ninja movie with the famous actor Sonny Chiba.

Ph. Hatsumi began studying martial arts at the age of seven and quickly reached the rank of instructor of Judo, Kendo, Karate and Aikido and Kobudo expert until he became a direct student of Takamatsu Toshitsugu, going to him every weekend by train more than 1300 km just to study with him, this for fifteen years, while during the week he worked in his clinic as a chiropractor. Before the death of Grand Master Toshitsugu, on 2 April 1972, Masaaki Hatsumi, despite his young age, became his successor and heir of the schools:

34th Soke	Togakure Ryu Ninpo Taijutsu	戸隠流忍法体術
28th Soke	Gyokko Ryu Koshijutsu	玉虎流骨指術
28th Soke	Kukishin Ryu Happo Bikenjutsu	九鬼神流八法秘剣術
26th Soke	Shinden Fudo Ryu Dakentaijutsu	神傳不動流打拳体術
18th Soke	Koto Ryu Koppojutsu	虎倒流骨法術
18th Soke	Gikan Ryu Koppojutsu	義鑑流骨法術
17th Soke	Takagi Yoshin Ryu Jutaijutsu	高木揚心流柔体術
14th Soke	Kumogakure Ryu Ninpo Taijutsu	雲隱流忍法体術
15th Soke	Gyokushin Ryu Ninpo Taijutsu	玉心流忍法體術

Soke Masaaki Hatsumi was awarded with the Japanese Culture prize "Higashikuni no Miha" 東久邇宮文化褒賞, founded in April 18, 1963. This award has only one class, and can be awarded to men and women for contributions to the arts of Japan, of literature or culture. The prize is awarded on the Culture Day (November 3rd) of each year at the Higashikuni no Miha Palace.

Soke Takamatsu Toshitsugu
宗家 高松寿嗣

Kuri Gaeshi technique 栗返し performed by Soke Takamatsu Toshitsugu.

The Takamatsu's family was originally from Matsugashima in Ise. Takamatsu's father received the Shugendo temple of Kumano's master degree. The greatest wish of his father was that Toshitsugu become a military, so his father sent him to train with his uncle and martial arts teacher Toda Shinryuken Masamitsu. Since that day Takamatsu was sent to his uncle's Dojo of Shinden Fudo Ryu Jutaijutsu, Toda Shinryuken Masamitsu was a famous martial artist who taught at the military academy of Nakano. At 13 Takamatsu received the Menkyo Kaiden 免許皆伝 (the certificate of complete knowledge of traditional martial art) in the school of Shinden Fudo Ryu. Giving the master's degree certificate to young students was not usual, because it was necessary to achieve a high level of skill, to have the Master recognize the student is ready for it. After this school, his uncle taught him Koto Ryu, Togakure Ryu, Kumogakure Ryu, Gyokko Ryu and Gyokushin Ryu.

In 1900 Takamatsu Sensei went to the English school and the school of Georg Bundow and the classical Chinese school in Kobe. In that time he became member of the Dojo of Takagi Yoshin Ryu school, where Mizuta Yoshitaro Tadafusa was the 15th Soke.

When Takamatsu was 17 years old, a new security chief came to his father's factory, an elderly man who was famous in Japan for his skill in martial arts, called Ishitani Matsutaro Takekage. Normally he used an old Bokken made of oak as a walking stick. Ishitani was also given a small area of the factory to be used as a Dojo. With other people Takamatsu profit by the opportunity to study under the old Master. From him Takamatsu learned the school of "Kukishin Ryu Happo Bikenjutsu". Ishitani also knew various Ninjutsu arts. Ishitani taught at Takamatsu other two schools of which he was Soke. These were Takagi Yoshin Ryu (a different branch of the previous school that Takamatsu had already learned from Mizuta), and Gikkan Ryu Koppojutsu.

Takamatsu during the Second World War went to China and did several jobs, including teacher of martial arts, in fact he taught the Japanese martial arts at the English school, he got more than 1,000 students at the English school, and for this reason he was continually challenged by others martial arts instructors. Takamatsu's diary states that in China he won 12 deadly fights, and 7 matches.

Hanbojutsu no Kigen
半棒術の起源
(Origins of the Japanese short stick art)

It is said that the art of short stick fighting that is called in Japanese Hanbojutsu 半棒術, was born when the lances of the warriors were broken in the middle of the battle, which cleverly used the remaining half of the spear in combat. Later from the techniques of Hanbo were developed the techniques of the concealed blade stick called Shikomi-Zue 仕込み杖.

It is said that the techniques of Hanbojutsu have existed since the ancient of Japanese history, for example, when Yamato Takeru No Mikoto fought against Izumo Takeru, it is said that Yamato Takeru No Mikoto defeated Izumo Takeru with a stroke with the end of the short stick.

In the Bujinkan Dojo the techniques of the Hanbojutsu come mainly from the Kukishin Ryu 九鬼神流 school of the Kuki 九鬼 (Nine Demons) family. Many schools or Ryu-Ha 流派 are connected to the "Kuki" family that originated from the Clan Nakatomi (Fujiwara).

A famous member of the Fujiwara clan was Fujiwara No Kamatari that in the year 645 during a rebellion was the decisive force that brought the end of that war.

The 38th emperor Tenchi gave to him the secret scrolls "Amatsu Tatara Hibun" 天津蹈鞴秘文, as reward and to educate him to the new position of Prime Minister. This scrolls contains information to govern efficiently and to maintain the peace in the nation.

Amatsu Tatara 天津蹈鞴 can be translated as: Amatsu 天津: Divine Residence or the place where deities resides; Tatara 蹈鞴: The highest principles of nature which are the greatest secrets of the martial arts Bumon 武門 and spiritual teachings Shumon 宗門. The oldest symbols of these scrolls are more than 2500 years old, around this period of time, a group of Malaysians, Tibetans, Chinese and Koreans escaped from their country, and went to Japan. These people brought with them the manners, philosophy, martial skills, writings and medical knowledge that were slowly assimilated into Japanese culture.

In the year 607, (after Christ) Nakatomi Kamatari, together with the emperor Tenchi, killed the powerful leader of the Soga family that had the Japanese imperial court totally under his control. As a reward, Kamatari became a Shogun, and in this role began the reform of the Taika era (645) and established the central government in Japan.

In the year 669, Nakatomi Kamatari assumed the surname Fujiwara and became the founder of the Fujiwara-Shi 藤原氏 clan that dominated Japan from the ninth to the eighteenth century.

The Fujiwara clan reigned for more than 600 years, thanks to the knowledge of the Amatsu Tatara Hibun, they gave origin to the Shinden Fujiwara Muso Ryu 神傳藤原無双流, from which the Kukishin Ryu school originated.

In the Kukishin Ryu school there is the legend of how the Hanbojutsu techniques were born in this school, when one of its members Ohkuni Taro Takehide met in the battlefield Yashiro Gonnosuke Ujisato, the spear of Ohkuni was broken in two during the battle, he using the broken staff of the spear knocked down Yashiro.

Kuriyama Ukongen Nagafusa developed the Hanbojutsu techniques of the Kukishin Ryu school, these resume by Ohkuni Kogenta Yukihisa that created the Jojutsu 杖術 techniques (4 feet long stick art Yonshaku 四尺 about 120 cm) starting from the knowledge of Hanbojutsu 半棒術 (short stick techniques), Rokushaku Bojutsu 六尺棒術 (long stick techniques), and Kenpo 剣法 (ancient sword art).

三心の構

SANSHIN NO KAMAE
(Postures of the three hearts)

In the oldest scrolls of the Kukishin Ryu school called Shinden Amatsu Tatara Ryu Hanbojutsu 神伝天津蹈鞴流半棒術 which are based on the Amatsu Tatara Kangi Den 天津蹈鞴槓技伝 scrolls there are described three postures in Japanese Kamae 構 that are; Kata Yaburi, Munen Muso and Otonashi. These are collectively called Sanshi Den 三志伝, Sanshin no Kamae 三心の構 and Sanso no Kata 三想の型. Grandmaster Takamatsu Toshitsugu used the term Sanshin no Kamae 三心の構.

Kata Yaburi no Kamae　　**Munen Muso no Kamae**　　**Otonashi no Kamae**
型破の構　　　　　　無念無想の構　　　　　音無の構

Kata Yaburi no Kamae
型破の構
(Breaking the form posture)
"The attitude of breaking the form."

Also called Hira Ichimonji no Kamae 平一文字の構, Kachimi 勝身の構, Kata Yaburi no Kokoro 型破の心.

To assume the position properly keep your spine straight, feet open as wide as shoulder's height, holding the stick with both hands horizontal to the ground, as Kokoro Gamae 心構え mental attitude you must be relaxed, but always alert, must be a spiritual vigilance, does not have to transpire nothing from the facial expression or from the position of the body. The advantage of this position is that it does not alert the opponent.

Kata Yaburi no Kamae Yori no Bo
型破の構えよりの棒

(Striking with the stick from the posture Kata Yaburi no Kamae Mugamae 型破の構無構 "Posture without posture breaking the form").

Sukui Uchi
すくい打ち
(Spoon strike)

From Kata Yaburi no Kamae advance with the left foot hitting from bottom to the top with the left end of the Hanbo hitting Gedan 下段 (low), Chudan 中段 (middle) or Jodan 上段 (high) with Uchi Age 打ち上げ (striking upward) or Hane Age 跳ね上げ.

Hane Age 跳ね上げ hitting to Jodan 上段.

Uchi Age 打ち上げ hitting to Gedan 下段.

Han Gaeshi Uchi
半返し打
(Strike with half rotation)

From Kata Yaburi no Kamae move slightly to the side and throw the stick with your left hand, rotate it to 180 degrees in the right hand, striking the opponent's wrist by grabbing the stick with the left hand.

Katate Furi
片手振り
(One-handed swing)

From Kata Yaburi no Kamae keeping the posture look to the left going into Yoko Ichimonji no Kamae 横一文字の構 (changing the grip of the right hand), advance with the right foot and leaving the grip with the left hand use the weight of the stick to make a Furi 振り swing from the bottom to upward by hitting at the left vital point called Kasumi 霞 from above (hit by holding the stick with the inverted grip called Gyakute 逆手).

Munen Muso no Kamae
無念無想の構

(Without mind without thoughts posture)
"The attitude to be free of all thoughts that distract the mind."

This position is also called Tate no Kamae 立の構え, Shinsen no Kamae 神仙の構, Mushin no Kokoro 無念の心, Mushin no Kamae Mugamae 無心の構え無構え, Shizen no Kamae 自然の構え.

To assume the position properly keep your spine straight, feet open as wide as shoulder's height, holding the stick with the right hand on the right side like a walking stick, as a mental attitude Kokoro Gamae 心構え you must be relaxed, mindless, mind is always ready for a possible attack from any direction because it does not fix on a particular thought, thus maintaining the state of Mushin 無心. The advantage of this position is that you give to the opponent the feeling that you are not on guard, but looks like you'r just walking around.

Munen Muso no Kamae Yori no Bo
無念無想の構えよりの棒
(Hitting with the stick from the posture without mind and without thoughts)

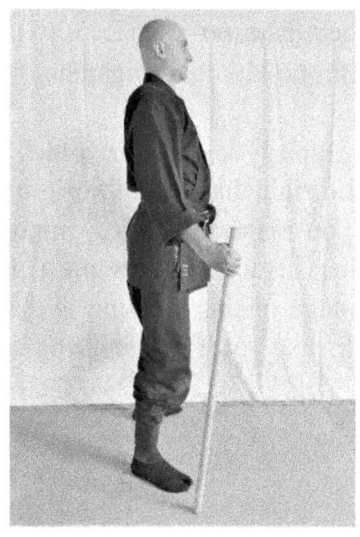

Tate Tobi
楯飛び
(Shield jump)

From Munen Muso no Kamae jump high, in the air hit with one hand swing with the stick, "Kukan de no Katatefuri" 空間での片手振 (Swing with one hand in the space), to perform this technique it is important to train in the Taihenjutsu 体変術 "Techniques of body movement" of the Shiho Tenchi Tobi 四方天地飛び "jumping in the four directions heaven and earth".

Migi Hachiji Katate Furi
右八字片手振り
(Eight shape swing with the right hand)

From Munen Muso no Kamae swing the stick in the shape of Hachi 八 (8 in Japanese) with the right hand, drawing in the air the sign of infinity ∞.

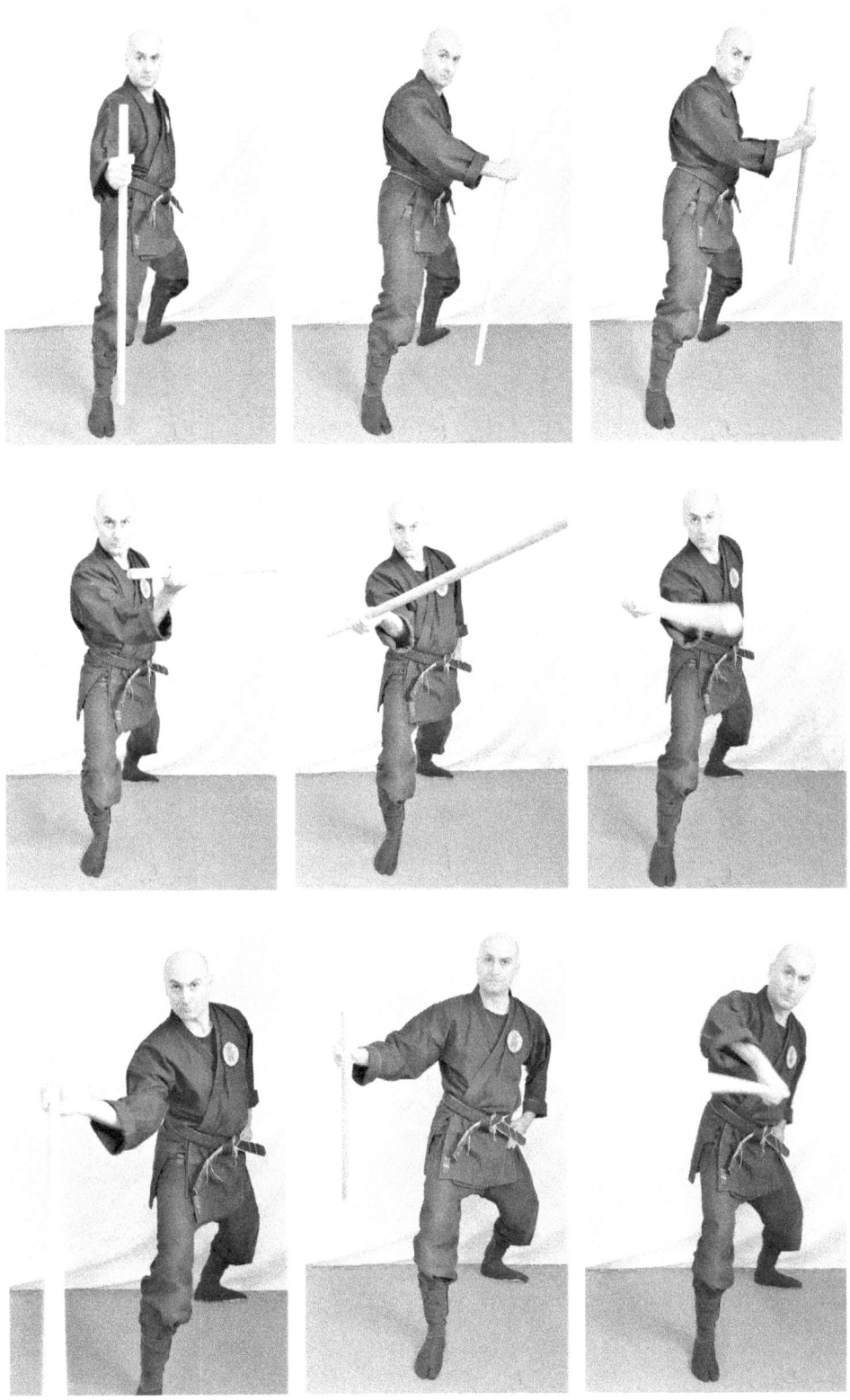

Tsuki Gaeshi
突き返し
(Reversal thrust)

From Munen Muso no Kamae wrap the stick with the arm bringing it under the armpit and strike with the tip of the stick stepping with the right foot, rise the stick and grab it with the left hand and stepping back with the right foot to hit the right vital point Kasumi, swing the stick with the right hand, turning it in the left hand to strike with a blow to the opponent's Kote.

Tsuki Do Furi
突き胴振り
(Tthrust and torso swing)

From Munen Muso no Kamae wrap the stick with the arm bringing it under the armpit and strike with the tip of the stick stepping with the right foot, immediately leave the stick from under the armpit grabbing it with the left hand and hit the trunk on the left Hidari Do Uchi 左胴打.

(Detail of the thrust with the stick).

Katate Furi Men Uchi
片手振り面打
(Strike the face with one handed swing)

From Munen Muso no Kamae stepping with the right foot striking with a Furi from the bottom to upward sideways at the left vital point Kasumi, grabbing the stick with the left hand and strike in the vital point called Tento 天頭.

Henka Katate Furi Men Uchi
変化 片手振り面打
(Strike the face with one handed swing, variation)

From Munen Muso no Kamae stepping with the right foot striking with a Furi from the bottom to upward at the vital point called Asagasumi 朝霞, grabbing the stick with your left hand hitting at the vital point called Tento 天頭.

Tokikaku Uchi
頭鬼角打ち

(Hit with the edge of the stick, called "Strike with the horn of the demon")
You can use the edge of the tip of the stick or its edge to hit different points and in different ways such as:

Strike the fist with the edge of the stick, Uchi Harai 打払.

Strike with Tokikaku Uchi at the vital point Jakkin, Jakkin Uchi 弱筋打.

Strike with Tokikaku Uchi at the vital point Tento, Tento Uchi 天頭打.

Strike with Tokikaku Uchi at the vital point Yaku, Yaku Uchi 扼打.

Strike with Tokikaku Uchi under the right cheekbone, Migi Kenkotsu Uchi 右顴骨打.

Strike with Tokikaku Uchi at the vital point Asagasumi, Asagasumi Itto Uchi 朝霞一当打.

Painful compression with the edge of the stick's tip on the bones, Kotsu Itami Dori 骨痛捕り.

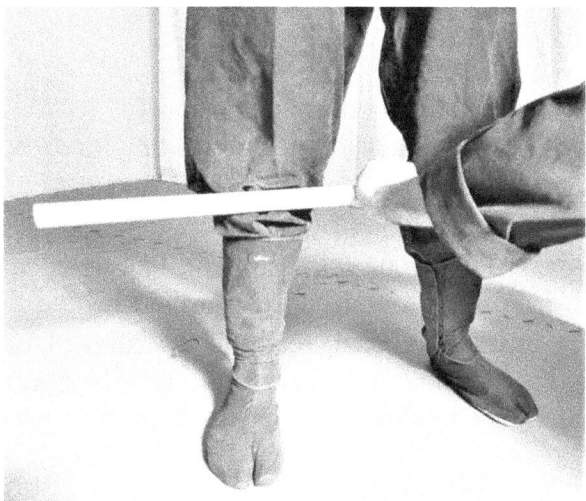

Holding the stick in the center, strike the opponent's shinbone with the stick's edge, Ryo Ashi Uchi 両足打.

Hit the face and abdomen with the edge of the stick vertically, Tate Uchi 立打.

Otonashi no Kamae
音無の構
(Without sound posture)
"The attitude of not saying anything and waiting for an opportunity."

Also known as Danpi no Kamae 断飛の構, Kage no Ippon 影の一本, Otonashi no Kokoro 音無の心, Otonashi no Kamae Mugamae 音無の構無心.

To assume the position properly keep your spine straight, feet open as wide as shoulder's height, holding the stick with both hands horizontally to the ground behind the back, as mental attitude Kokoro Gamae 心構え you must be relaxed, ready to hit but without showing your intentions, without involuntarily telling the opponent what we want to do. The advantage of this position is that you can attack or counterattack the opponent in ways that are unexpected to him, and to surprise him.

Otonashi no Kamae Yori no Bo
音無しの構えよりの棒
(Strike with the stick from the without sound posture)

Otonashi no Kamae Katate Furi
音無しの構え片手振り
(Without sound posture one-handed swing)

From Otonashi no Kamae let go the grip with your left hand and hit from the bottom to upward by shifting the weight of the body to the left.

Kuri Gaeshi
栗返し

("Reversal chestnut" also called Kachiguri no I 勝栗の意 Idea of dried chestnut)

From Otonashi no Kamae rotate the wrist bringing the tip of the stick over the right shoulder and strike the vital point Tento.

KISO
(Foundation; basis)

The techniques that are called "basis" in Japanese Kiso 基礎 are very important and should be trained in a constant way no matter what degree you have, in fact some individuals are affected by the Dunning-Kruger effect which is a cognitive distortion due to which individuals little experts in a field tend to overestimate their abilities, thinking wrongly to be experts in the field, this is why we must always keep humble and train even in basis techniques. In martial arts as in any other art it is important to maintain a constant training not only to improve and refine one's skills, but also to keep the skills acquired. Very often, most people tend to procrastinate, so it is important to train using the principle Kaizen 改善 (improve) which, as Soke Masaaki Hatsumi says, consists in training effortlessly to improve, very often people think they should start a workout with hard training from the beginning it will be unproductive, this because the people are in a hurry to get results, the important thing is to have patience and train step by step creating healthy habits, to be able to improve day after day.

Akuheki
"You must abandon the bad habits to become good."

Masaaki Hatsumi

Keri
蹴り
(Kicks)

From Munen Muso no Kamae kick with the stick in your right hand, training to kick forward, backward, to the right and to the left Shiho Geri 四方蹴.

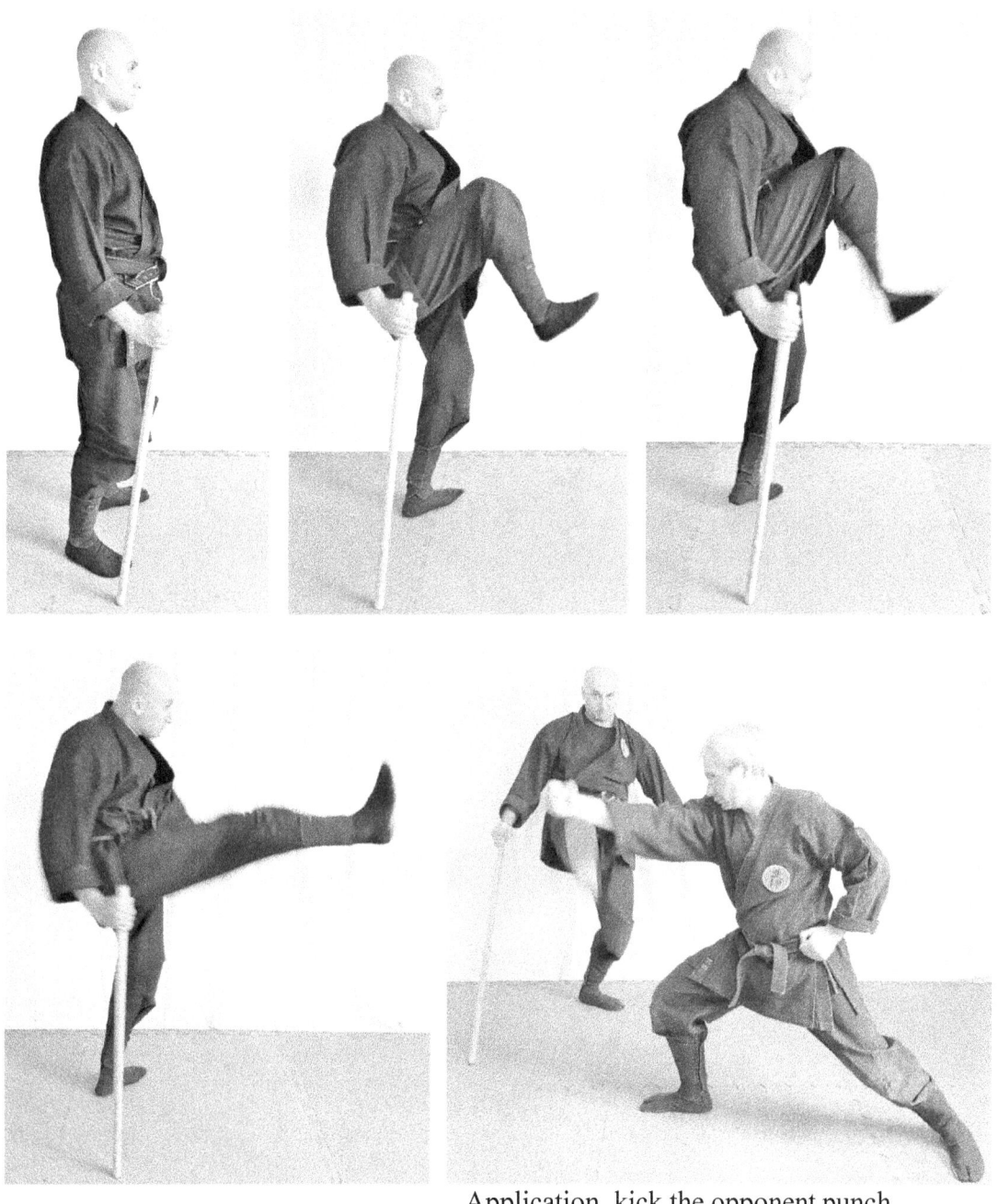

Application, kick the opponent punch.

Sanshin no Taihen
三心の体変
(The three hearts movement of the body)

Starting from any Kamae train to develop body movement by bending on the knees, flexing backwards and then bending forward. Tai no Furi Tsuki 体の振り突き (Thrust with body swing). Shin 心 (Heart or Mind) by Sanshin can also be written with the ideogram for "Furi" 振 (Swing).

Kyuho Uchi
九法打ち
(Nine methods of striking)

From Kata Yaburi no Kamae practice Hiza Uchi 膝打, Do Uchi 胴打, Kasumi Uchi 霞打, Tento Uchi 天頭打, Uchi Age 打ち上げ and Tsuki 突. Also called Uchi Waza 打技 (Hitting techniques).

Hiza Uchi 膝打 practice hitting the left and right knee (also called Sune Uchi 脛打).

Do Uchi 胴打 practice hitting the torso left and right (also called Waki Uchi 脇打).

Kasumi Uchi 霞打 practice hitting the left and right temple (also called Yokomen Uchi 横面打).

Tento Uchi 天頭打 hit in the vital point above the head (also called Men Uchi 面打).

Uchi Age 打ち上げ (also written 打揚) hit in the groin (you can also hit with Hane Age 跳ね上げ also written 跳擧).

Tsuki 突 hit with a thrust the vital point called Suigetsu.

Taihenjutsu
体変術

(Techniques of body movement)

The practice of falls and rollings are essential in martial arts, for this reason you must be able to do it with a weapon in your hands. Practice falls and rollings with a stick in your hands.

UKEMI GATA 受身型 (Form to receive with the body)

Zenpo Kaiten 前方回転 Forward roll.

Sokuho Kaiten 側方回転 Sideways roll.

Tate Nagare 立流れ Stand up flow.

Gyaku Nagare 逆流れ Twist flow.

Yoko Nagare 横流れ Sideways flow.

Junagare 順流れ Flowing in the opportunity, roll diagonally.

Taisabaki Gata
体捌き型
(Form of the body movements)

Practicing the defensive body movements hitting with the stick avoiding the attacks inside Ura 裏 and outside Omote 表.

Naname Ushiro Ura Waki Uchi
斜め後ろ裏脇打

Naname Mae Omote Waki Uchi
斜め前表脇打

Mawashi Kote Uchi Ura
廻し小手打裏

Kote Uchi Omote
小手打表

Katate Tsuki
片手突

Sabaki Dori

捌き捕り

(Avoid and catch)

Avoid the punch by striking the opponent's torso with the stick and grab the wrist, Ura 表 inside and Omote 表 outside (this basic movement is used to perform techniques such as Tsuke Iri or Koshi Ori and many others).

Sabaki Dori Ura
捌き捕り裏

Sabaki Dori Omote
捌き捕り表

Ashi Dori
足し捕り
(Leg capture)

The opponent strikes with a right front kick, from Kata Yaburi no Kamae avoid outside and hitting with the right tip inside the opponent's right ankle, as he lays his leg on the ground hit with the left tip of the stick making pressure to bring the opponent to the ground, control the opponent by putting pressure with the stick over the knee and on the right elbow joints.

Sankaku Jime
三角締め
(Triangle strangling)

Kubi 首

The strangling techniques are very dangerous, and you should be very careful in practicing them, you have to start with light pressure and increase it gradually, you must NEVER bring your partner in the unconscious state, you should practice them under the supervision of your teacher that should know the basic techniques of first aid, or the traditional Japanese techniques called Kappo 活法 or Katsu 活 "resuscitation techniques".)

Tekubi 手首

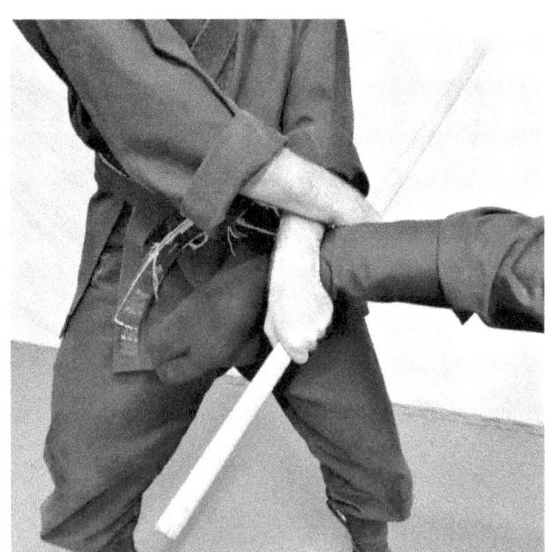

Ashikubi 足首

Shime Tejun
締め手順

(How to put the hands for the strangles)

Hand positioning methods in the use of Sankaku Jime:

Ryotenouchi Uchi Mukou 両掌内向こう Both palms down.

Kousa 交差 Inverted palms.

Ryotenouchi Soto Mukou 両掌外向こう Both palms upward.

Katate Buri
片手武利

(One handed swing, the ideogram for swing Furi 振り can also be read as Buri, is replaced with the ideograms for martial Bu 武 and advantage Ri 利)

From Munen Muso no Kamae practice the following strikes from this position by swinging the stick with one hand.

Asagasumi Uchi 朝霞打ち

Kinteki Uchi 金的打ち

Hidari Kasumi Uchi 左霞打ち

Hadome Uchi 歯止打ち

Migi Kasumi Uchi 右霞打ち

Ashi Harai 足払い

Ryo Ashi Harai 両足払い

Kaze Harai 風払い

Katate Kakae Bo
片手抱え棒
(Embrace the stick with one hand)

The opponent hits with a right fist, from Munen Muso no Kamae avoid outside and embrace the stick under the arm hitting with the tip the vital point Uko 雨戸, or hit the vital point with a thrust, or strike with an ascending thrust Hanetsuki 跳突き.

Uko Uchi 雨戸打ち

Asagasumi Tsuki 朝霞突き

Asagasumi Hane Tsuki 朝霞跳突き

Furi Tsuki

振り突き

(Swing thrust)

The opponent attacks with a right fist, from Kyo Migi Jodan no Kamae 虚右上段の構え avoid outside and receive by striking with the tip of the stick to the Jakkin, grab the other end with the left hand and hit the right vital point Koran 虎乱.

Soe Te Uchi
添手打
(Striking by accompanying/deflecting the hand)

The opponent attacks with a right fist, from Munen Muso no Kamae change to Tenchi Furi no Kamae 天地振りの構え and hit from the top to the bottom at the Jakkin, from here you can do Ashi Barai 足払, Do Uchi and Tsuki, and other variations.

Henka 変化 Variation:
The opponent attacks with a right fist, from Munen Muso no Kamae avoid inside and grabbing the final end with the left hand hit the opponent's arm from the bottom deflecting it by turning the opponent, hit the shoulder downward, and press with the right knee on the opponent's right leg bringing him to the ground.

Kote Gaeshi Uchi
小手返し打ち
(Reverse strike on the wrist)

The opponent attacks with a right fist, from Munen Muso no Kamae place the stick on the left arm and control the opponent's fist by lowering it, insert the stick between the legs and grab it with the left hand and by pulling, the opponent falls down, control with Sokkotsu Ori.

Ate Gaeshi Ichi (Uchi Taoshi)
当返し一 (打ち倒し)

(Reverse strike; one, also called "Striking and knocking down")

The opponent attacks with a double grab to the lapel, from Kata Yaburi no Kamae take a step back with your right foot while arching your back slightly backwards to strike under the opponent's arms, then step forward with your right foot bringing the left foot back doing a Tsuki at the vital point Suigetsu 水月 or perform a Tate Uchi 立打 (strike with the stick in vertical) over the forehead.

Tate Uchi 立打

Ate Gaeshi Ni

当返し二

(Reverse strike; two)

The opponent attacks with a right kick, from Kata Yaburi no Kamae anticipate by advancing slightly outside and hit the opponent's right shinbone of kicking leg just by slightly raising the stick, kneel on the left leg and hit the left opponent's knee with the right tip.

Ate Gaeshi San
当返し三
(Reverse strike; three)

The opponent attacks with a right kick, from Kata Yaburi no Kamae anticipate by advancing directly with the right foot and striking the opponent's kick just by slightly raising the stick, hit with the left tip inside the right thigh and then the left thigh, kneeling on the left leg to hit the inside of the right knee to make the opponent fall down, control him by squeezing the right ankle with the stick.

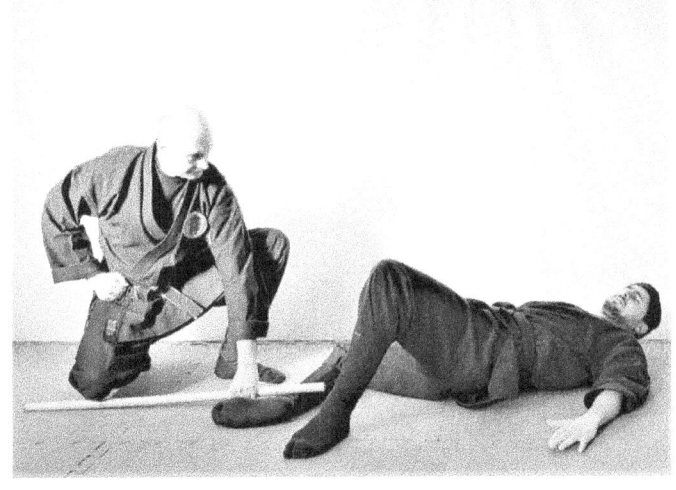

KIHON HAPPO
(Eight basic methods)

The Kihon Happo 基本八法 is a basic form from the school Gyokko Ryu Koshijutsu, and consists of the Koshi Sanpo No Kata 骨指三法の型 "The three methods of striking with the fingers bones form", and Torite Goho No Kata 捕手五法の型 "Five methods of capturing the arm form". It is said that if you are not able to master this form your martial arts skills will not be good enough. It is also said that the myriad techniques of the martial arts were born from these eight basic techniques.

It is said that if you are not able to master this form your martial arts skills will not be good enough. It is also said that the myriad techniques of the martial arts were born from these eight basic techniques. The Kihon Happo is not limited to the Kihon Happo of the Gyokko Ryu Koshijutsu, but there is a dormant inside all the nine schools. Learning the Kihon Happo, followed by the techniques of the Juppo Sessho as a self-defense tool, you can also learn the use of the knife, the gun and waking up to Sanshin no Kata in the three directions using the blinding powder, the Shuriken, and the stones, as well as the art of short stick. This to be able to develop the basic feeling of the "real combat" Jissen 実戦.

Training the Kihon Happo and its endless variations Banpen Henka 万変変化, not only with bare hands but also with weapons, takes years of practice to fully understand it. There must be balance in conscious and unconscious training, not focusing only on training the technique itself, but also in its variants, otherwise you can never understand the deeper principles of Budo, this way the martial arts are maintained alive and always actual. In fact, the real Kihon Happo is something alive, think of one of the basic teachings of Buddhism "The impermanence of all things", in fact all things change continuously and nothing is permanent. The techniques shown below come from the Taijutsu hand-to-hand combat of the Kihon Happo – Torite Goho no Kata and its variants applied to the use of short stick Hanbo.

Taijutsu

"If you can only perform the Taijutsu 体術 (bare hand combat), but you can't use weapons, you will never really understand (the Budo). Taijutsu represents the first third of what we study. The study to use weapons as a natural part of Taijutsu represents the remaining two thirds."

Masaaki Hatsumi

Omote Gyaku Dori

表逆捕り

(External twist capture)

The opponent grabs the right end of the stick with his right hand, rotate the stick counterclockwise by placing the Omote Gyaku joint-lock, to avoid that the opponent lets go the grip, grab his hand or his fingers with your right hand while maintaining the grip of the stick.

Omote Gyaku Uko Dori
表逆雨戸捕り
(External twist rain door capture)

The opponent grabs the right wrist with his left hand, turn the stick clockwise to put Omote Gyaku, rotate the end to hook the wrist and with the other end hit the right side of the opponent's neck to the vital point called Uko, with the right hand put Omote Gyaku pressing with the stick on the neck throwing the opponent to the ground and control with the joint-lock.

Omote Gyaku Asami Dori
表逆狭み捕り
(External twist hold capture)

The opponent grabs the right wrist with his left hand, turn the stick clockwise to hook the wrist, then pass the left hand under the opponent's wrist grabbing the end of the stick to do a Sankaku Jime on the wrist and with the other end hit the right side of the opponent's face, press with the stick throwing the opponent to the ground and control with the joint-lock.

Hongyaku
本逆

(Regular joint-lock)

The opponent with his left hand grabs the left end of the stick, rotate the stick clockwise to do the Hongyaku joint-lock.

Hongyaku Dori (Bo Gaeshi)
本逆捕り (棒返し)

(Regular joint-lock capture, also called "Reverse stick")

The opponent grabs the left end of the stick with his right hand, turn the stick clockwise to do the Hongyaku joint-lock, to prevent the opponent from releasing the grip, grab the opponent's fingers while keeping the stick's grip with the left hand.

Ura Gyaku Gata
裏逆型
(Internal twist form)

The opponent grabs the left end of the stick with his right hand, rotate the stick clockwise to do the Ura Gyaku joint-lock grabbing the opponent's hand, as practiced in Taijutsu (hand-to-hand combat), from this technique you can do endless variations together with Hanbo techniques.

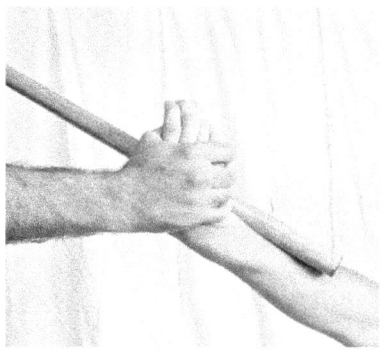

A) Eri Jime 襟締め (Strangulation with the collar).

B) Katate Nage 片手投げ (One handed throw).

C) Ryoashi Dori 両足捕り (both legs capture).

Ura Kote Gaeshi
裏小手返し
(Internal wrist reversal)

The opponent grabs the right wrist with his left hand, from Kata Yaburi no Kamae turn the stick counterclockwise and put the Ura Gyaku joint-lock, while the opponent lose the hold, take his left hand holding it into Ura Gyaku, hit with the stick to the trunk and do Tsuke Iri always keeping the Ura Gyaku joint-lock, control him.

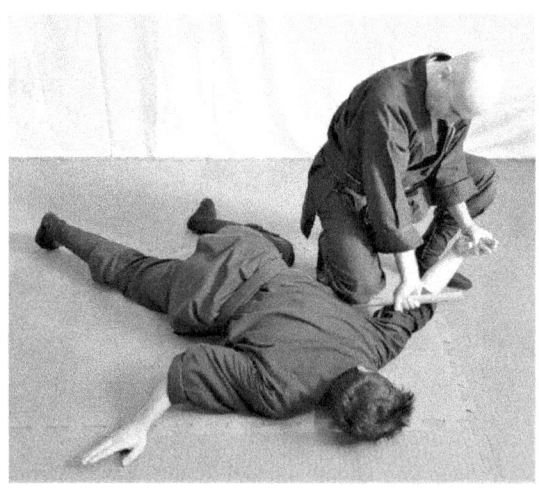

Take Ori
竹折り
(Break the Bamboo)

The opponent grabs the right end of the stick with his left hand, rotate the stick counterclockwise to do the Take Ori joint-lock with the tip of the stick under the wrist.

Take Ori Kata - Kobushi Dori
竹折型-拳捕り
(Break the Bamboo form - Fist capture)

The opponent grabs the right end of the stick with his left hand, turn the stick counterclockwise to do the Take Ori joint-lock with the tip of the stick under the wrist, continuing the rotation to bring the opponent to the ground using the joint-lock.

Musha Dori
武者捕
(Warrior capture)

The opponent attacks with a right fist, from Kata Yaburi no Kamae avoiding the punch inside performing Mawashi Kote Uchi Ura, from this position using the left end of the stick and the elbow wrap the opponent's arm counterclockwise, while moving sideways and behind him and perform the joint-lock to his arm.

Juji Dori Ichi
十字捕り一
(Cross capture; one)

The opponent with his right hand grabs the left arm, from Munen Muso no Kamae take a step back with the left foot placing the stick under the opponent's right arm, putting pressure under his elbow putting his arm in the lever until he stands on the tiptoes for the pain.

Juji Dori Ni
十字捕り二
(Cross capture; two)

The opponent does Kumiuchi 組打, he grabs the lapel with his left hand and with his right the sleeve of the left arm, from Kata Yaburi no Kamae insert the left end of the stick into the arms of the opponent, placing the stick over his right arm and pressing under the left elbow with the central part of the stick performing Juji Dori while putting Ura Gyaku on his left hand, from this position pass the stick under his left arm and over his neck, and then with your left hand grab the left end to the side of the opponent's neck to perform a choke, control.

Oni Kudaki Dori
鬼砕き捕り
(External demon smash capture)

The opponent attacks with a right fist, from Kata Yaburi no Kamae perform Naname Ushiro Ura Waki Uchi, insert the stick between the opponent's triceps and forearm, blocking with the left arm the opponent right wrist, once got the joint-lock with a rotated step backwards bring the opponent down to the ground and control him by keeping the joint-lock.

Oni Kudaki Henka
鬼砕き変化
Variants types of Oni Kudaki, details:

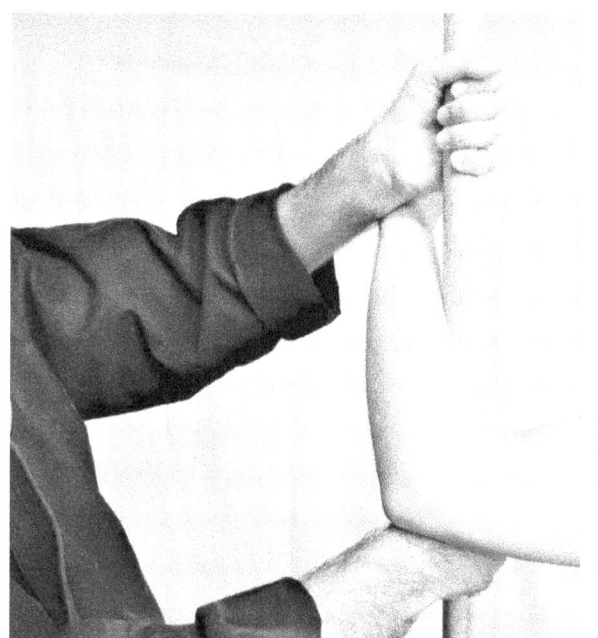

Omote Oni Kudaki
表鬼砕き
External demon smash

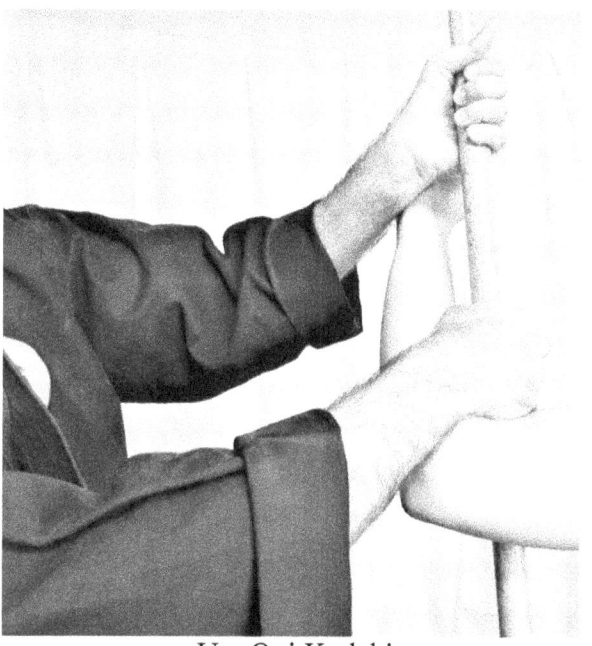

Ura Oni Kudaki
裏鬼砕き
Internal demon smash

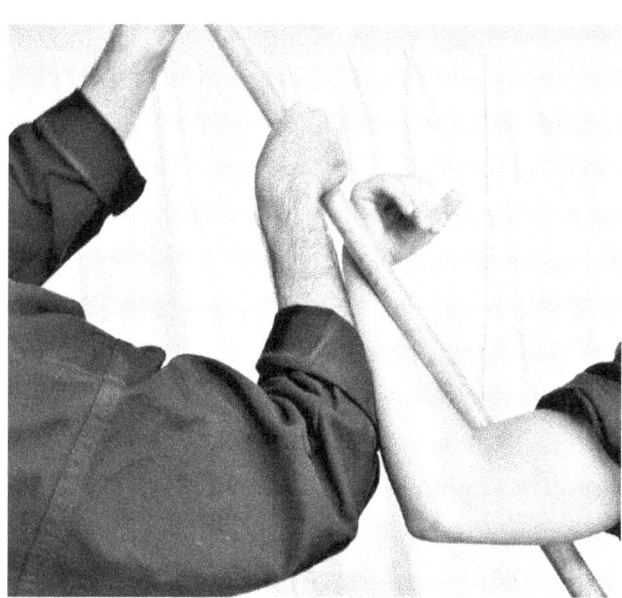

Tsuke Oni Kudaki
付け鬼砕き
Join demon smash

Omote Gyaku Yori Oni Kudaki
表逆より鬼砕き
Demon smash from external twist

Ashi Oni Kudaki / Sokki Kudaki
足鬼砕
(Leg demon smash)
Perform Onikudaki at the opponent's leg.

Omote Ashi Oni Kudaki
表足鬼砕き
Outside leg demon smash

Ura Ashi Oni Kudaki
裏足鬼砕き
Inside leg demon smash

Ashi Kudaki Yori Henka
足砕きより変化
(Variation from leg smash)

The opponent attacks with a right kick, from Kata Yaburi no Kamae block the opponent's shinbone between the right thigh and the right forearm, from here kneeling on the left leg and letting go the grip with the left hand hit the calf of the standing leg with the left end of the stick, take the left end of the stick with the left hand, than place the right end of the stick under his knee and with a rotation of the stick push on his leg to throw the opponent down.

Ganseki Nage

巖石投

(Throwing the big rock)

The opponent attacks with a right fist, from Kata Yaburi no Kamae perform Naname Ushiro Ura Waki Uchi, insert the stick under the triceps of the opponent's right arm, then insert your left leg between his legs, turn your trunk to throw him.

Ganseki Otoshi

巖石落

(The big rock fall)

The opponent attacks with a right fist, from Kata Yaburi no Kamae perform Naname Ushiro Ura Waki Uchi insert the stick under the triceps of the opponent's right arm, then insert your left leg between the legs of the opponent, as to perform the technique Ganseki Nage, the opponent resist, suddenly lower on the right knee and push with the stick forward and downward, block the opponent's right leg with your left leg and knock him down.

Ganseki Otoshi Makikomi

巖石落巻込

(The big rock fall wrapping up)

The opponent attacks with a right fist, from Kata Yaburi no Kamae perform Naname Ushiro Ura Waki Uchi, insert the stick as for Ganseki Nage. As the opponent resists, release the grip with the right hand and grab the upper end, rotate your left wrist to bring a lever to the opponent's elbow and pull it to bring the opponent to the ground, kneeling on the left leg, the opponent will slam his face against your right knee.

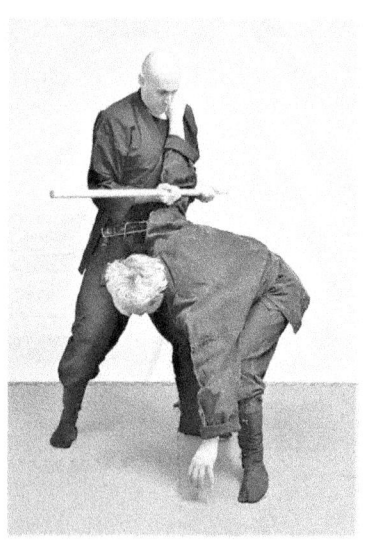

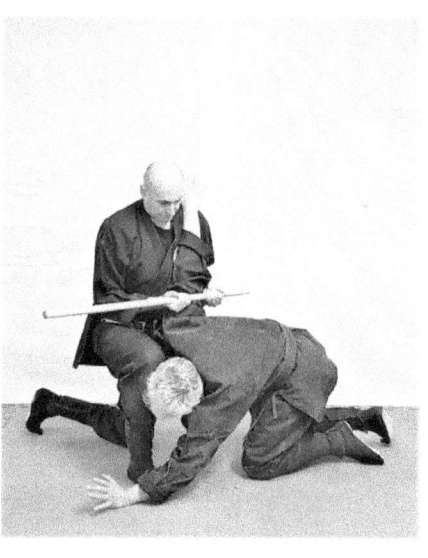

Ganseki Otoshi Garami (Makiage)
巖石落搦(巻き上げ)
(The big rock fall binding, also called "To roll up")

The opponent attacks with a right fist, from Kata Yaburi no Kamae perform Kote Uchi Omote then lock the opponent's arm between the stick and your left arm wrapping the opponent's arm from the bottom to up, bringing the opponent's arm behind his back and control with the joint-lock to his shoulder.

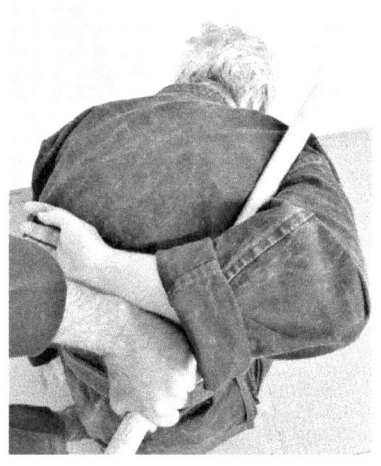

Control variation; Tsuki in the vital point Butsumetsu 仏滅

Control variation; bring the opponent to the ground and lock the wrist with your left hand, in this position you can also defend from another opponent.

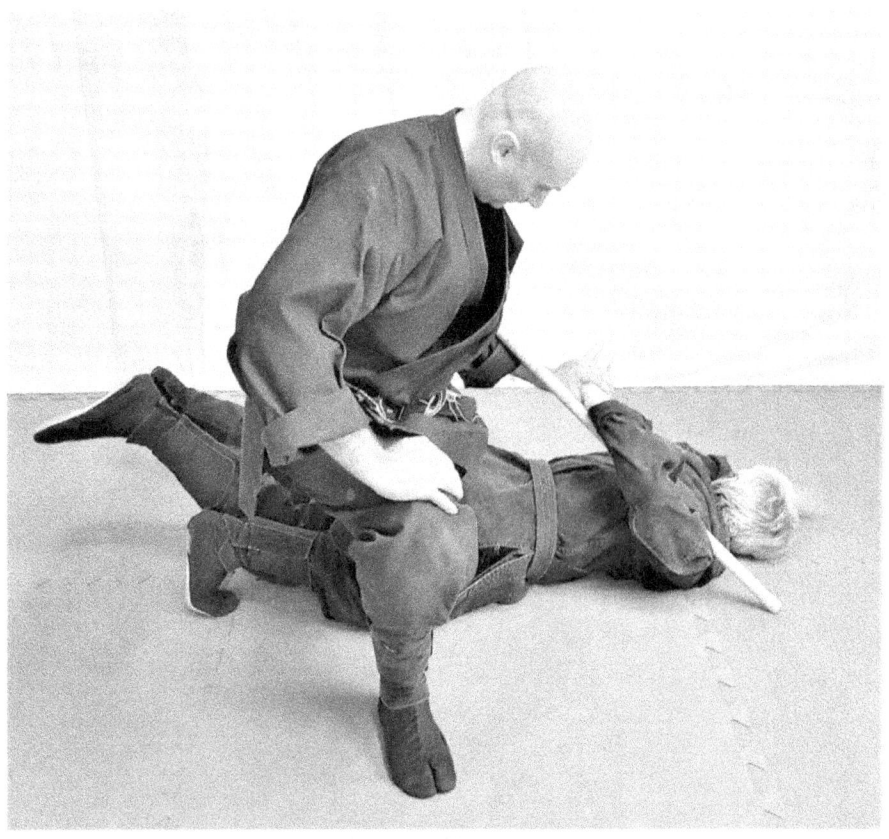

Ude Garami Omote

腕絡み表

(Tie up the arm, external)

The opponent attacks with a right fist, from Kata Yaburi no Kamae avoid outside let the grip go with your left hand, you absorb the fist with Nagashi Uke 流し受け hook the fist between your right wrist and the end of the stick, grab the right end of stick with your left hand to perform a Sankaku Jime on the opponent's wrist performing a painful clamp control.

Gyaku Ude Garami

逆腕絡み

(Reverse tie up the arm)

The opponent attacks with a hook punch, from Kata Yaburi no Kamae avoid outside striking with the right end of the stick under the opponent's triceps. The opponent closes his arm to block the stick, suddenly leave the grip with your left hand and grab the part of the stick above the opponent's arm, rotate the stick behind the opponent's back and put his shoulder in a joint-lock, control the opponent.

Muso Dori
武双捕
(Capture martial pair)

The opponent grabs your left arm with his right hand, from Kata Yaburi no Kamae pass the stick under the opponent's right elbow, let the stick go with your right hand, grab it again over the opponent's elbow, turn clockwise the stick, take a step backwards to put his arm in a lever and by kneeling on the left leg, the opponent slam his face on your right knee.

Jigoku Dori Ichi
地獄捕り一
(Hell capture, one)

The opponent grabs your right arm with his left hand, from Munen Muso no Kamae perform a lever by passing the stick under the opponent's left elbow, grab the upper end of the stick with your left hand, and push the lower end of the stick inside the opponent's left knee to bring him to the ground, control with the lever on his arm.

Jigoku Dori Ni

地獄捕り二

(Hell capture, two)

The opponent grabs your right arm with his left hand, from Munen Muso no Kamae perform a lever passing the stick under the opponent's left elbow and grab the upper end of the stick with your left hand, press the lower end of the stick inside his left knee, grab the end of the stick from behind his knee with your left hand and control the opponent.

投げ型

NAGE KATA
(Throw form)

空間
Kukan

"To throw someone, you must control the Kukan, bring the opponent to the point where it is easy to throw him. When you throw someone, take him to the point where he falls easily. In this way he will throw himself, please play with the Kukan to discover this point."

Masaaki Hatsumi

Katate Nage

片手投

(One handed throw)

The opponent attacks with the Kodachi and performs a thrust, from Kata Yaburi no Kamae you avoid outside and grab the opponent's wrist with your right hand, and with your hand strike with the left end of the stick to his neck, raise his arm and pass under it to throw him by twisting his wrist.

Morote Nage (Awase Nage)
諸手投げ(合わせ投げ)

(Two-handed throw, also called "Join together throw")

The opponent grabs the end of the stick with both hands, in harmony with the opponent's strength redirect it in order to throw him; use his right hand as fulcrum, turn the stick counterclockwise over his head to throw him. You can grab his fingers or press with your fingernail on the opponent's fingers to avoid that he let go the grip of the stick.

Morote Otoshi
諸手落とし
(Two-handed drop)

The opponent grabs the end of the stick with both hands, using the opponent's right hand as the fulcrum rotate the stick counterclockwise over his head and place your right leg behind his right leg, to make the opponent's fall down to the ground, from here control the him pushing the tip of the stick on his throat, if he tries a kick hit with the stick inside of his right thigh and then his ankle of the foot that kicks.

Uchimata
内股
(Inner thigh)

The opponent attacks with a left fist, from Kata Yaburi no Kamae perform Naname Ushiro Omote Waki Uchi and grab his left wrist with the right hand, insert the right end of the stick between the opponent's right arm and his legs, put his arm in lever between the stick and your right side, move forward and to the side to kick inside the opponent's left thigh to throw him.

Hane Kurui

跳ね狂い

(Lunatic leap)

The opponent attacks with a right fist to the abdomen, from Munen Muso no Kamae avoid outside and strike by wrapping the stick and the opponent's arm under your arm hitting his trunk, with the left foot sweep from the inside the opponent's right foot to make him fall to the ground, if the opponent reacts do a thrust.

Gaeshi Do
返し胴
(Reversal trunk)

The opponent attacks with a right fist, from Munen Muso no Kamae perform a Jodan Nagashi Uke 上段流し受け (it is not a parry, you absorb the fist by sliding it on your forearm deviating it) raising the opponents arm and then hit his torso with the stick, pass the stick under the arms to perform a Dojime 胴締, compressing the opponent's last ribs, insert yours hips and throw him with a inverted hips throw; Harai Goshi Gyaku Otoshi 払腰逆落.

Tomoe Nage
巴投げ
(Comma throw)

The opponent grabs the stick with both hands and pushes forward, from Kata Yaburi no Kamae, lock the opponent's hands and use his push to perform Tate Nagare by placing the sole of your right foot on his hip to throw him over you.

Tomoe Gaeshi Ashi Dori Osae
巴返し足捕り押さえ
(Comma throw control with the capture of the legs)

The opponent grabs the stick with both hands and pushes forward, from the position Kata Yaburi no Kamae take advantage of his push action to perform Tate Nagare and by placing the sole of the foot on his left hip to throw him, but the opponent avoids the throw, from this position on the ground hold the grip with the right hand and with the left hand pull the his ankle in order to make him fall to the ground. With your right hand that hold the stick turn it to put the opponent's hand in Ura Gyaku, and with your left arm wrap his left foot and place it in a joint-lock.

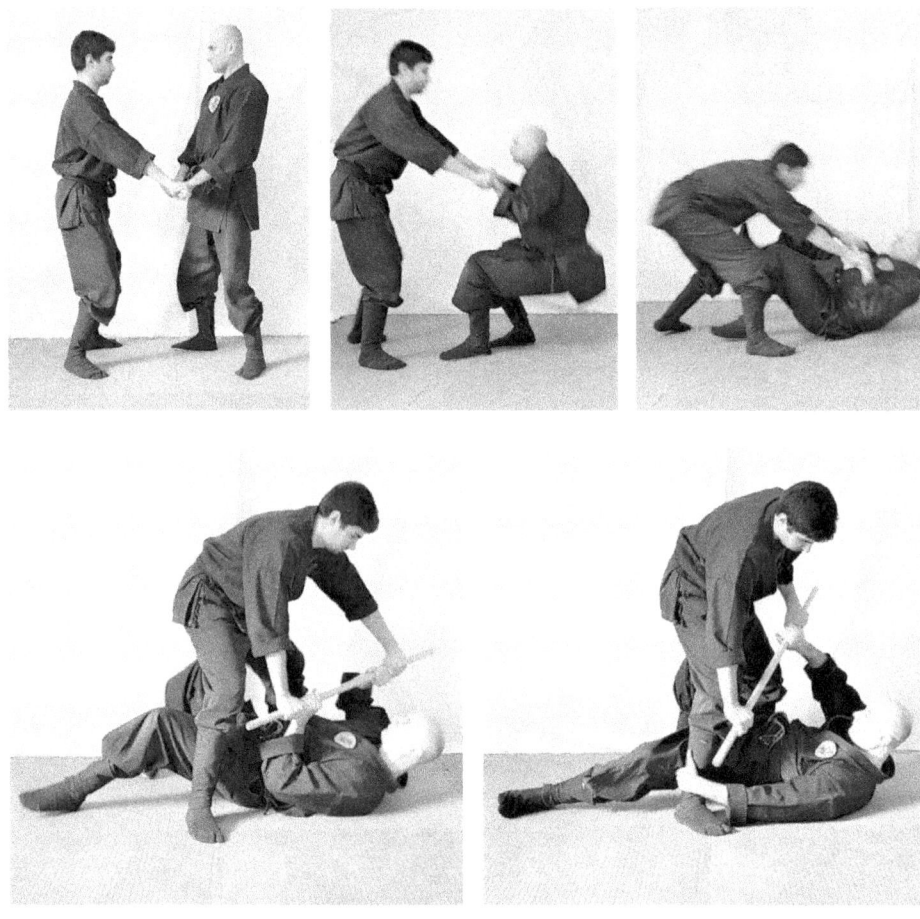

胸捕り型

MUNA DORI KATA
(Lapel grabs form)

間合い
Maai
"You must learn to use the space between you and the opponent, the distance is very important!"
Masaaki Hatsumi

Katate Dori

片手捕り

(One hand grab)

The opponent grabs the collar with his left hand, from Kata Yaburi no Kamae slide the stick into his right hand let the grip go with your left hand and place the left end of the stick over the opponent's wrist, with the left hand grab the stick and perform Kotsu Itami Dori (painful bone capture), and bring the opponent face down to the ground.

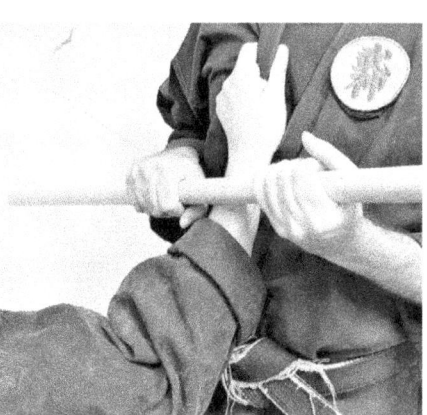

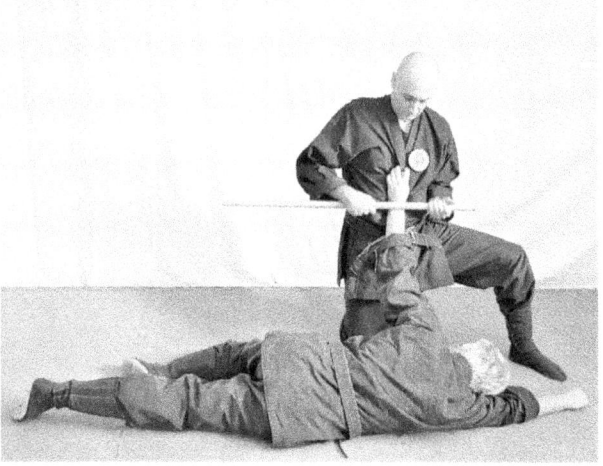

Hiki Otoshi

引き落とし

(Pulling down)

The opponent grabs the lapel with his right hand, from Munen Muso no Kamae perform a Sankaku Jime on the opponent's wrist with the stick, pulling down bring the opponent to the ground.

Karame Dori
搦め捕り
(Binding capture)

The opponent grabs the lapel with his right hand, from Kata Yaburi no Kamae perform a Sankaku Jime to the opponent's wrist with the stick and lower him, release the grip with your right hand, letting the stick go to hit his head, grab the stick again with your right hand to the side of the opponent's head, to perform a Shime with the stick and the arm.

Hiki Otoshi
引き落とし
(Pulling down)

The opponent grabs the lapel with his right hand, from Munen Muso no Kamae perform a Sankaku Jime on the opponent's wrist with the stick, pulling down bring the opponent to the ground.

Karame Dori
搦め捕り
(Binding capture)

The opponent grabs the lapel with his right hand, from Kata Yaburi no Kamae perform a Sankaku Jime to the opponent's wrist with the stick and lower him, release the grip with your right hand, letting the stick go to hit his head, grab the stick again with your right hand to the side of the opponent's head, to perform a Shime with the stick and the arm.

Ryote Karame (Ryote Garami Dori)
両手搦め (両手絡み捕り)

(Tie both hands, also called "Tying both hands capture")

The opponent performs a double grab to the collar, from Kata Yaburi no Kamae imprisoning both wrists of the opponent with Sankaku Jime perform with the stick a Kotsu Itami Dori, enter with your hips to levering his arms, from this position you can control through the lever or throw him.

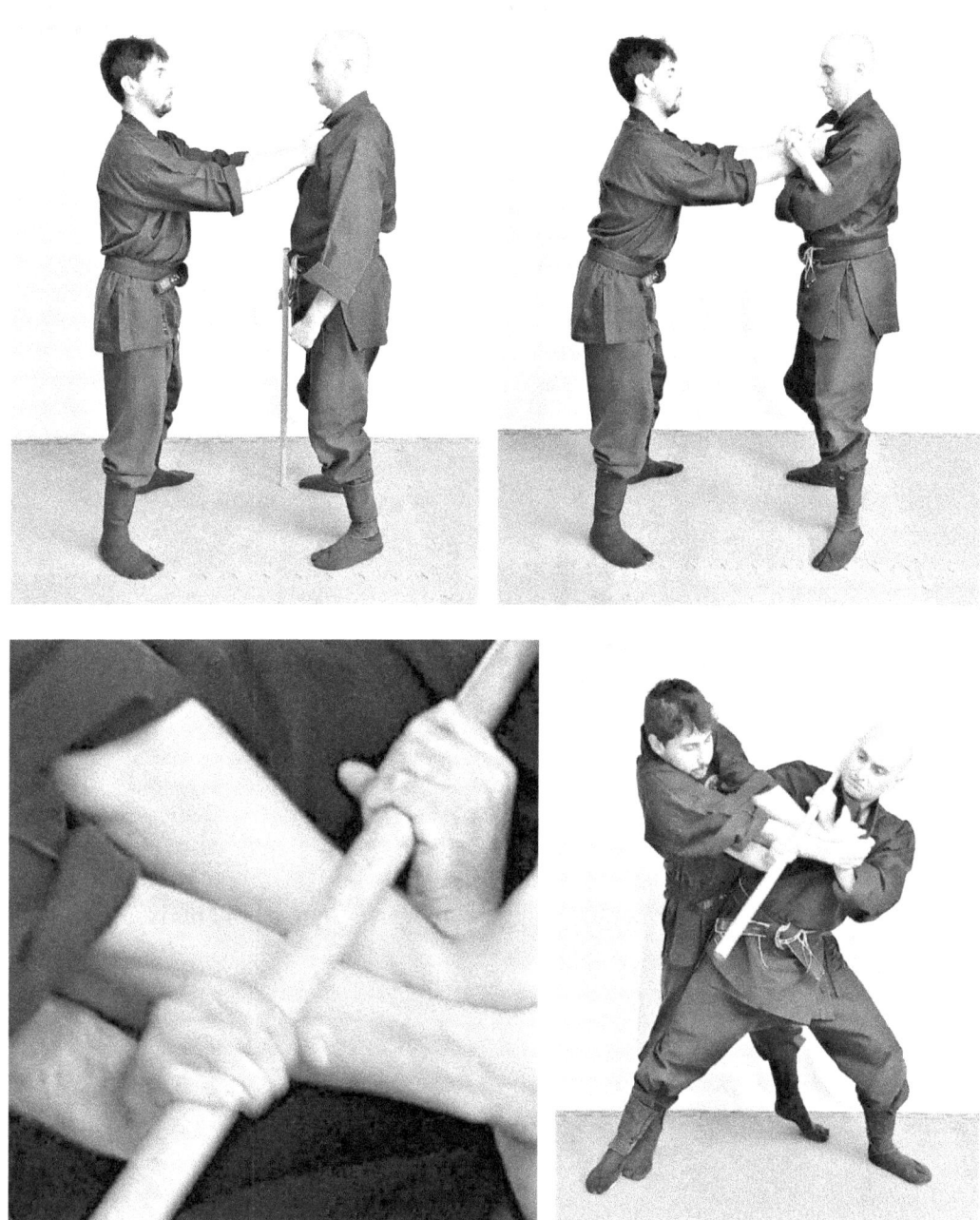

手解き型

TEHODOKI KATA
(Free the hands form)

動き
Ugoki
"It's not just your hands, you have to move your whole body."

Masaaki Hatsumi

Kote Gaeshi
小手返し
(Twisting the wrist)

The opponent grabs the right wrist with his left hand, from Kata Yaburi no Kamae take a step backwards with your left foot, you turn the stick to the outside of the opponent's blocking hand with your left hand while pressing your thumb into his hand, perform the Ura Gyaku joint-lock pressing with the stick on the wrist's bone, from this grab control the opponent.

Kasumi Uchi
霞打ち
(Mist strike)

The opponent attacks by grabbing the right wrist with his left hand, from Kata Yaburi no Kamae, take a step back with your right foot and hit with the stick's left end at the opponent's vital point right side Kasumi. Stepping back with your left foot turn the right end of the stick clockwise so that you lay the right end of the stick over the opponent's wrist from this position leave the grip with your left hand and grab the stick passing the hand under the opponent's wrist grabbing the right end and performing a Sankaku Jime on his wrist, blocking it in a painful grip.

Ude Gaeshi
腕返し
(Twisting the arm)

The opponent attacks grabbing your right wrist with his left hand, from Kata Yaburi no Kamae, take a step with your right foot, let the stick go with your left hand and rotating the stick counterclockwise so as to place it over his wrist, from this position grab the stick again with the left hand by pressing on the wrist blocking it in a painful grip, kneel on your left leg pulling the opponent to the ground and control him.

Ryote Dori
両手捕り
(Capture both hands)

The opponent attacks by grabbing the wrists with both his hands, from Kata Yaburi no Kamae, let the stick go with your left hand and turning the stick clockwise, place it over the opponent's wrists from this position grab the stick again with your left hand, passing it under the wrists of the opponent, locking his wrists with Sankaku Jime in a painful grip.

後捕り型

USHIRO DORI KATA
(Grabs from behind form)

残心
Zanshin
"You should not think only of your opponent, you must control everything around you."
Masaaki Hatsumi

Ushiro Dori Dojime

後捕り胴締み

(Capture from behind tightening the torso)

The opponent grabs from behind at shoulder's level, from Kata Yaburi no Kamae lower your hips and free yourself by pressing below the elbow of the opponent with the left elbow, go behind the opponent and grab him with the stick and performing a Dojime put the shoulder behind the back and pull the stick to compress the opponent's abdomen, and put his arm in lever with your neck, control him.

Ushiro Dori Ashi Dori (Benkei Dori)
後捕り足捕り (弁慶捕)

(Capture from behind leg capture, also called "Shinbone capture")

The opponent grabs from behind, from Kata Yaburi no Kamae break the grabs of the arms by lowering your hips and raising your elbows, and inserting the stick behind the opponent's leg, grab the stick again and pull upwards, and sitting on his leg to make him fall down on his back, control him by keeping the lever on his leg.

Taiboku Taoshi
大木倒し
(Big tree knock down)

The opponent attacks from behind with a torso grip, from the posture Kata Yaburi no Kamae, hitting with your hips and your head backwards, than place one foot behind the opponent's legs and perform a Dojime with the stick on the ribs in the vital point called Butsumetsu. Quickly lower your body and pull the stick on both the opponent's legs, knock him down to the ground, control the opponent with an Itami Osae on his shinbones.

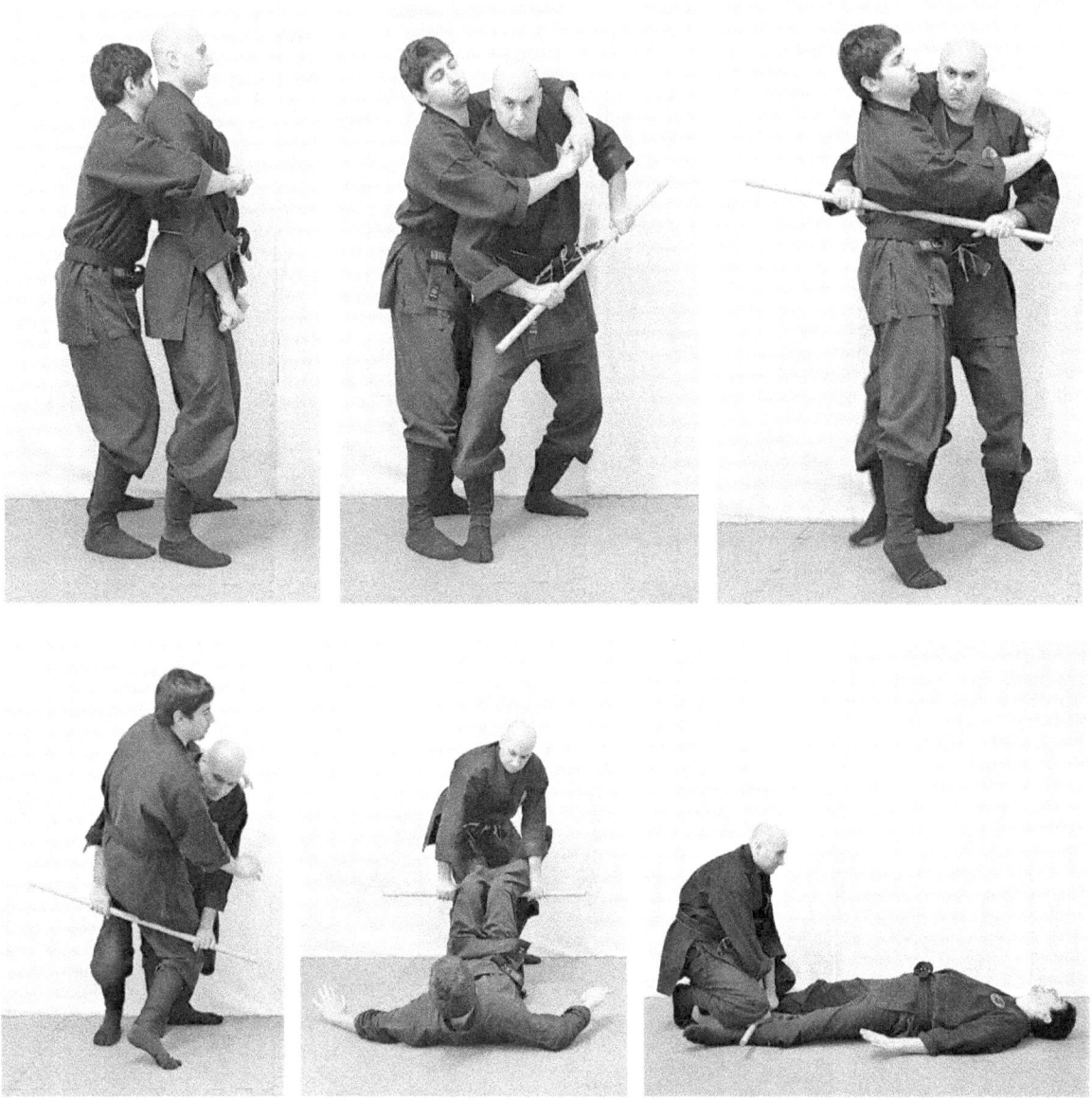

Tawara Taoshi
俵倒し
(Straw bag knock down)

The opponent attacks from behind with a torso grip, from the posture of Kata Yaburi no Kamae, let the stick go with the left hand, pass the stick behind the back of the opponent and grab it again with the left hand, from this position pull the stick to arching the opponent's back, once broken the grab perform any technique such as Tsuke Iri or Koshi Ori to bring the opponent to the ground.

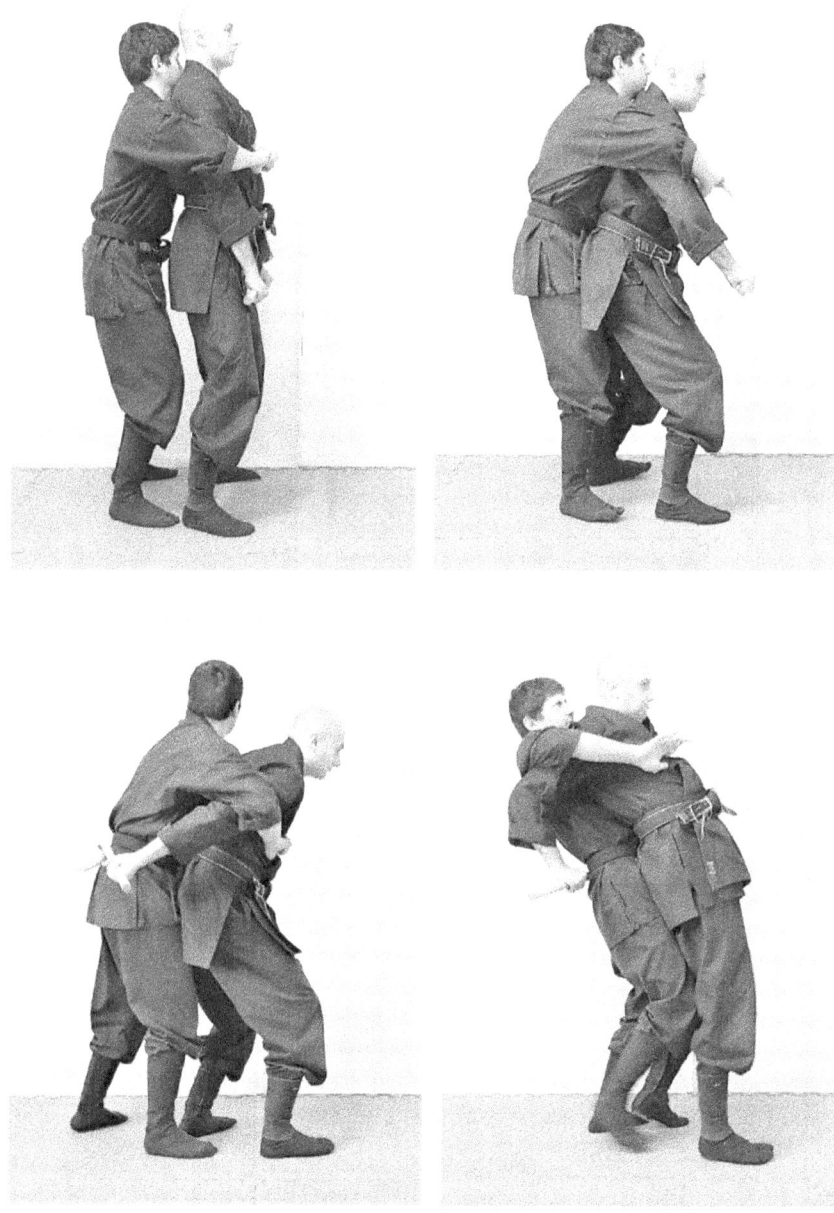

突き返し型

TSUKI GAESHI KATA
(Counterattack fist form)

小蝶
Kocho
"Avoid like a butterfly."

Masaaki Hatsumi

During his second trip in China the Soke Takamatsu, met Cho Shiro, a very strong and famous Shaolin Kung Fu warrior, Cho Shiro lifted a trunk more than 100 times every day as training, and he was the personal guard of Cho Sajurin, an important political figure, who was killed in an explosion during an attack. Cho challenged twice Takamatsu, Takamatsu twice didn't accept. One night, Takamatsu had a dream where a Kocho 小蝶 butterfly avoided all the attacks of a giant demon Oni 鬼 . The next day he was challenged again, this time Takamatsu accepted. In the fight, Takamatsu avoided all of Cho's attacks like a butterfly until Cho lowered his guard. At that moment the fight ended, from that moment Cho and Takamatsu became martial friends Buyu 武友.

Ate

当

(Hit)

The opponent attacks with a right fist, from Kata Yaburi no Kamae lower the body and hit upwards under the opponent's wrist with the center of the stick, perform a Kikaku Ken at the Butsumetsu, hit at the same point with the central part of the stick, and then perform a Sankaku Jime with the stick to the opponent's torso and control him.

Ryou Ashi Dori
両脚捕
(Both legs capture)

The opponent attacks with a right fist, from Kata Yaburi no Kamae raise the stick and strike down to the opponent's forearm, lowering his arm, letting the stick go with your left hand, and going behind him, grab the stick again, pull the ankles with the stick and push with the shoulder to knock down the opponent forward, control him by pressing with the stick on his ankles.

Kasumi Uchi
霞打ち
(Mist strike)

The opponent attacks with a right fist, from Kata Yaburi no Kamae hit the Kote with the right end of the stick deflecting the fist by shifting the weight of your body on the left leg, hit the opponent's right temple side with the left end of the stick. (Henka 変化 variation, directly hit the temple by placing the left forearm under the stick).

Henka 変化 variation.

Ashi Kudaki
足砕き
(Leg smash)

The opponent attacks with a right fist, from Munen Muso no Kamae lowering on your left knee (Moguri Kata 潜型) striking inside of his ankle with the stick's upper end , getting up by wrapping the opponent's arm and put the lower end of the stick behind his right knee, step on his foot, with the other hand grab the opponent's left arm by rotating it backwards from this position, you perform Ashi Ude Kudaki 足腕砕き break the opponent's leg and arm.

Muna Kudaki
胸砕き
(Chest smash)

The opponent attacks with a right fist, from Munen Muso no Kamae receive his punch performing Bokote Gaeshi 棒小手返し, passing the stick between the arm and behind the opponent's back and grabbing the other end of the stick, and place the left arm on the opponent's chest, from this position perform Do Jime.

Bokote Gaeshi 棒小手返し

Hagai Jime

羽交い締め

(Binding both wings)

The opponent attacks with a right fist, from Kata Yaburi no Kamae perform Naname Ushiro Omote Waki Uchi, with the right arm passing the stick under the opponent's right arm and moving it behind his neck, and with your other arm passing under his left arm to grab the end of the stick again, blocking his arms to make a compression on his neck with the stick (in training do not hurt the partner with the compression, you must apply a gradual pressure).

Kyoukotsu Kudaki

胸骨砕

(Breastbone smash)

The opponent attacks with a right fist, from Kata Yaburi no Kamae perform Naname Ushiro Omote Waki Uchi, let the stick go with your left hand and insert it between the opponent's torso and arm, go behind the opponent and grab the end of the stick again with your left hand and perform Do Jime with the stick, press in to the breastbone (in training do not hurt the partner with the compression, you must apply a gradual pressure).

蹴り返し型

KERI GAESHI KATA
(Counterattack kicks form)

足捌き
Ashisabaki

"The first thing you should think, is about the movement of the feet, the stick is secondary. If your movement of the feet is correct, the stick will follow naturally."

Masaaki Hatsumi

Ashi Kujiki

足挫き

(Leg crush)

The opponent attacks with a left front kick, from Kata Yaburi no Kamae one hand strike with the stick under the opponent's thigh, pass the stick under the opponent's leg blocking the ankle inside of your elbow, grab again the stick with your right hand in a painful grip on the opponent's ankle putting it in a joint-lock.

Ashi Kujiki Henka
足挫き変化
(Leg crush variation)

If the opponent has already put down the foot after the kick, kneel on your right leg and hit his back leg to the vital point Kaku, holding the stick with one hand, grab the end of the stick behind the opponent's knee and shifting the weight on your left knee put his leg in a joint-lock, control him.

Ashi Ori
脚折

(Breaking the leg)

The opponent attacks with a right front kick, from Kata Yaburi no Kamae avoid inside lowering your body, and let the stick go with your left hand grab the opponent's right ankle, with the stick hit inside of his left knee. Pass the stick over the opponent's right ankle, blocking it between the stick and your left wrist, place it in a joint-lock, and control.

Ashi Dori
足捕
(Leg capture)

The opponent attacks with a high front kick, from Kata Yaburi no Kamae avoid inside and with the left end of the stick hook the opponent's leg under his knee, turn your spine and push with the stick to throw the opponent to the ground.

Ashi Garami
足搦
(Leg tie)

The opponent attacks with a front kick at medium height, from Kata Yaburi no Kamae avoid the opponent's kick outside and hook his ankle with the right end of the stick and perform Sankaku Jime to the opponent's ankle.

Ashi Gatame
足固め
(Tie tightly the leg)

The opponent attacks with a front right pushing kick, from Kata Yaburi no Kamae take a step backwards with your left foot and hook the opponent's leg between the left end of the stick and your left wrist, grab the stick with your right hand to perform a Sankaku Jime, blocking the ankle between your wrists and the stick in a painful grip.

Otonashi

音無し

(Without sound)

The opponent attacks with a front right pushing kick at medium height, from Otonashi no Kamae avoid slightly outside putting the right end of the stick under the opponent's leg, and turning counterclockwise to knock down the opponent, block his ankle kneeling on it and make a thrust.

逮捕術

Taihojutsu
(Arrest technique)

手足
Teashi
"When you have a stick in your hand, do not forget that you have the other limbs."
Masaaki Hatsumi

Jowan Ori
上腕折り
(Upper arm break)

Press with your body weight with your right knee on the stick, holding the upper end of the stick with your right hand so it doesn't slip, pressing it on the opponent's triceps, while with your left hand pull the opponent's wrist upwards to put a lever on his arm.

Hiji Ori
肘折

(Elbow break)

Press with your body weight with your right knee on the Jujiro 十字路 Kyusho, holding the opponent's wrist with your left hand, while pulling with your right hand the stick that is under his triceps, to put in lever the opponent's elbow to break it.

Zenwan Ori
前腕折
(Forearm break)

Press with your body weight with your left knee on the stick that presses on the opponent's radio, while holding the stick with your right hand so it doesn't slip, with your left hand hold the opponent's wrist and press with the right tip of your right foot on his ribs to hold him still, to prevent his kicks.

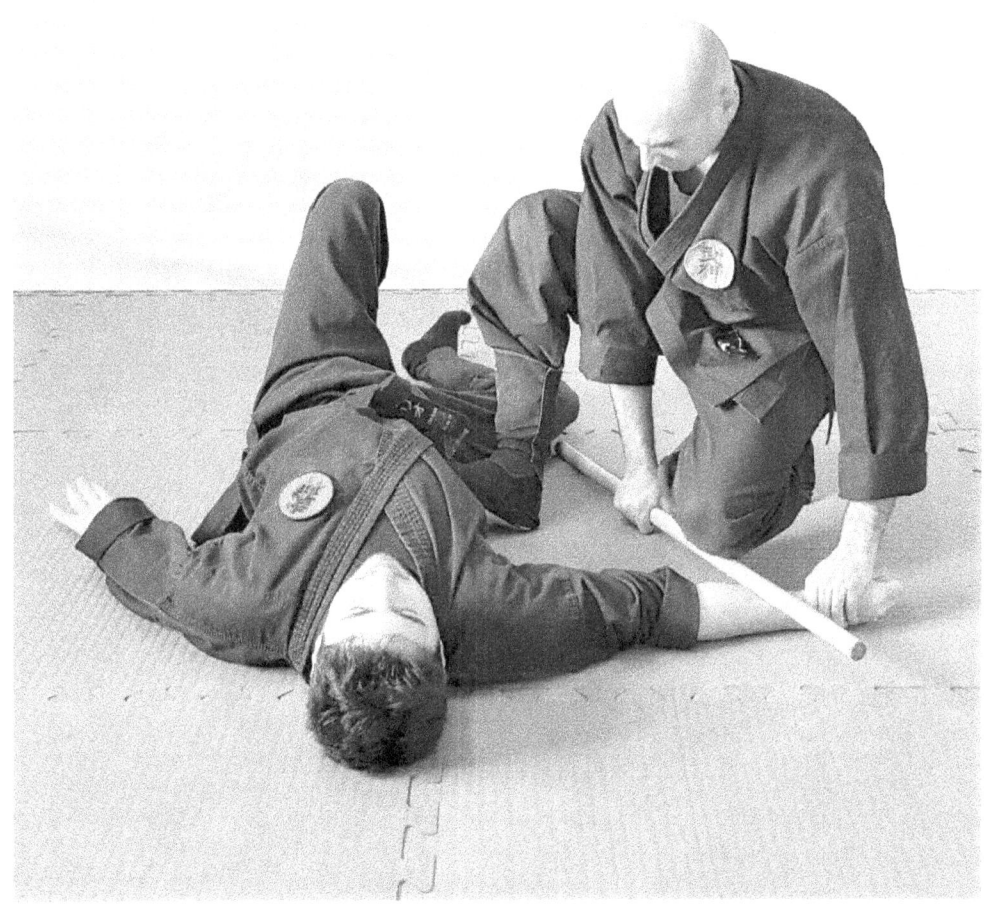

Sokkotsu Ori
足骨折
(Ankle break)

Press with your body weight with your right knee on the stick that presses behind the opponent's right ankle, while levering his left ankle with your left knee locking it between your left forearm and the stick with a painful pressure on his shinbone.

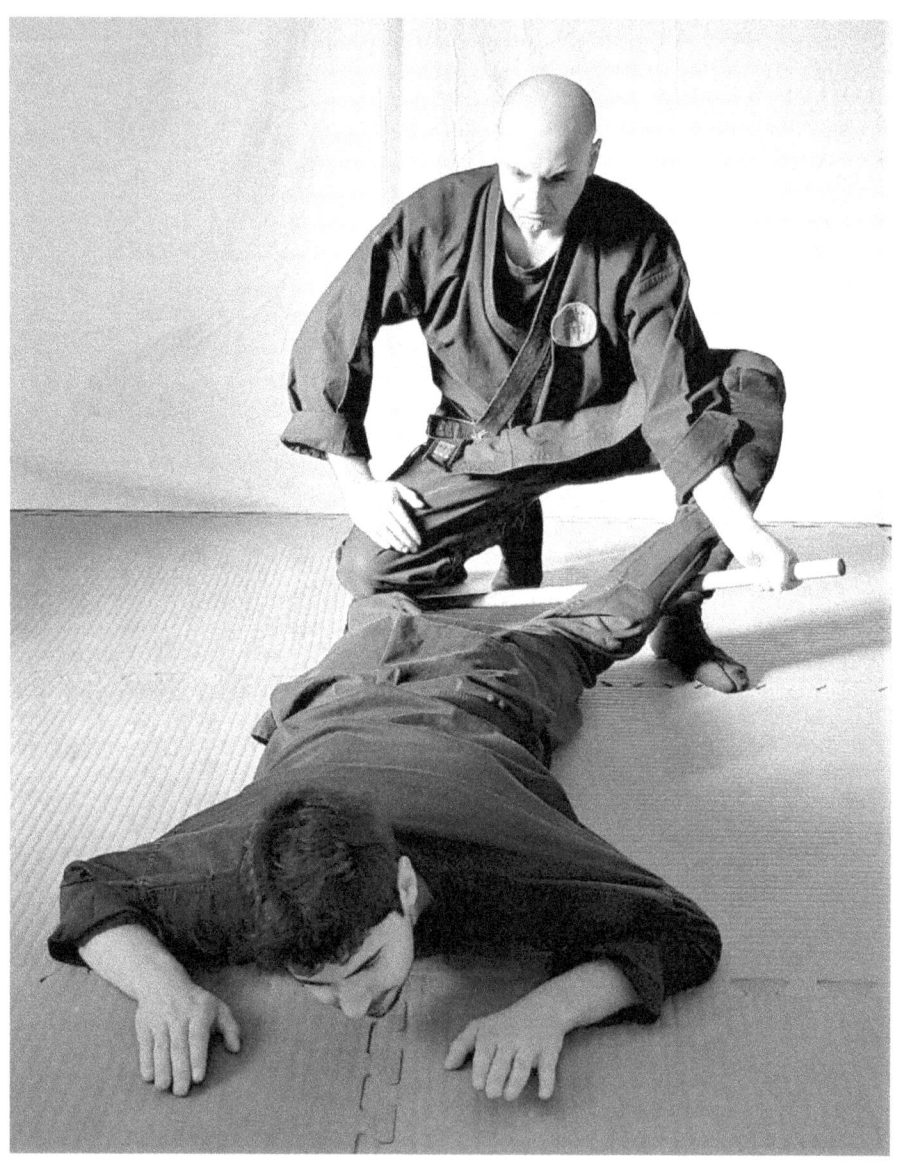

Ryote Ori
両手折
(Both arms break)

Press with your body weight with your left knee on the stick that presses on the opponent's right biceps, while your both the hands perform an Onikudaki joint-lock on the the opponent's left arm, at the same time apply a pressure in his throat with your left elbow.

Ogyaku
大逆
(Big reverse)

Insert the stick between the right side of the opponent's neck and his right arm by levering on his shoulder, pulling his right wrist with your left hand, while you block his left arm with your left leg.

Shintou

震盪

(Shock, concussion)

Sitting on the opponent's back blocking his arms with the stick pull arching his back, from this position you can kick the opponent's face or press the stick on his neck.

Itami Osae
痛み押え
(Painful pressure control)

The techniques known as Itami Osae 痛み押え are a kind of ground controls making pressure with the weight of the body in the vital points, muscles and bones Kotsu Itami Osae 骨痛み押え and it can also be combined with the joint-lock and levers, there are various applications:

Jakkin 弱筋

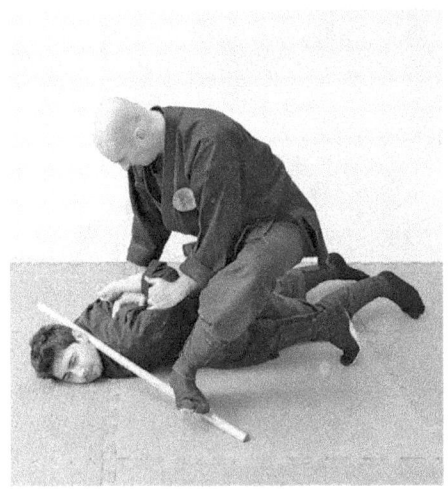

Kubi 首

Gaisai to Jakkin 外谷と弱筋

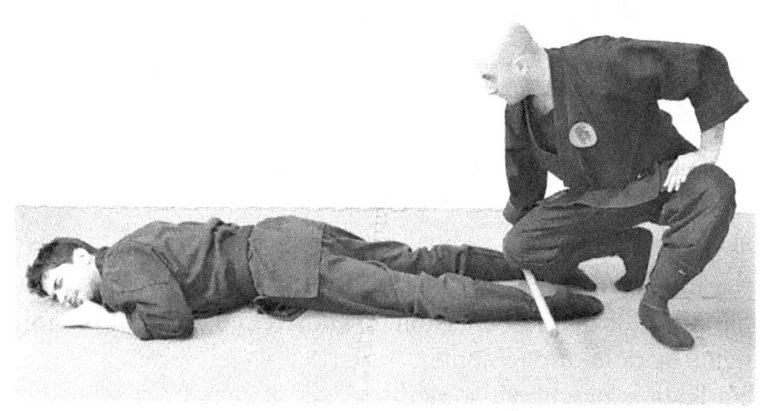

Ryo Ashikubi 両足首

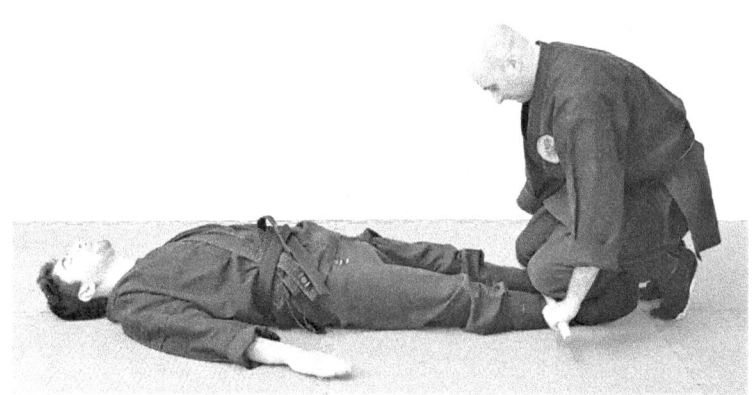

Ryo Benkei 両弁慶

Naisai Itami Osae Ashi Ori 内谷痛み押え足折

KATA TO KATACHI
(Form and Form)

The ideogram for Kata is formed by the radical Tsuchi 土 "Terrain" which is connected with Doji no Kami 土地の神 the divinity of the earth, to who were dedicated prayers to have benefits, here we see the divine inspiration for the transmission of knowledge through the imitation of the form or a sequence of movements or ritual movements.

No matter how much a Kata is practiced, something will always be missing, which is what is in its evolved form the Katachi 形, the Kata performed with feeling is the Katachi that goes beyond the physical qualities, the Katachi is the Kata with the soul, Kata can be taught Katachi not, it can be observed and experienced, and to do so you have to find the right teacher who can teach it, these terms are not only found in the martial arts, but also in the No theater, tea ceremony, Japanese dance etc.

It is said that in the No theater to learn the Katachi, one must steal the secret or the soul of the form by mastering the Kata, and in this way grasp the meaning for the Katachi. Understanding the feeling of the form and its meaning means truly mastering the "Form".

Tsuyoi

"Do not think that you are strong because you can do any technique well, do not be too full of yourself."

Masaaki Hatsumi

Tsuke Iri
附入り
(Enter and join)

The opponent attacks with a right fist, from Kata Yaburi no Kamae perform Naname Ushiro Omote Waki Uchi, and grab the opponent's wrist with your right hand, insert the stick between his torso and his arm, press the stick on his triceps with your body weight by stepping and bringing the opponent to the ground face down and control him by pressing the stick with your left knee.

Ushiro Dori Tsuke Iri
後ろ捕り付け入り
(Behind capture enter and join)

The opponent attacks from the back with a torso grab, from the posture of Kata Yaburi no Kamae, break the grab by hitting with the hips backwards and raising the arms, once broken the grab perform Tsuke Iri to bring the opponent to the ground.

Tsuke Iri Itto Dori
附入り一刀捕り
(Enter and join capture of the sword)

The opponent with the Kodachi performs a thrust, from Kata Yaburi no Kamae avoid at the outside striking the opponent's torso and perform the technique Tsuke Iri, disarm and control the opponent.

Koshi Ori

腰折り

(Hip break)

The opponent attacks with a right fist, from Kata Yaburi no Kamae perform Naname Ushiro Ura Waki Uchi, and grab with your left hand the opponent's wrist, insert the stick between his back and his arm, press the stick on his triceps with the weight of your body taking a step and bringing the opponent to the ground on his back, control him by keeping the right knee on the stick.

Shibari Koshi Ori
縛り腰折り
(Hip break binding)

The opponent attacks with a right fist, from Kata Yaburi no Kamae perform Naname Ushiro Ura Waki Uchi, and grab the opponent's wrist with your left hand, insert the stick between his back and his arm inserting it into his belt, press on his triceps and taking a step forward bring the opponent to the ground on his back, control him by keeping the right knee on the stick.

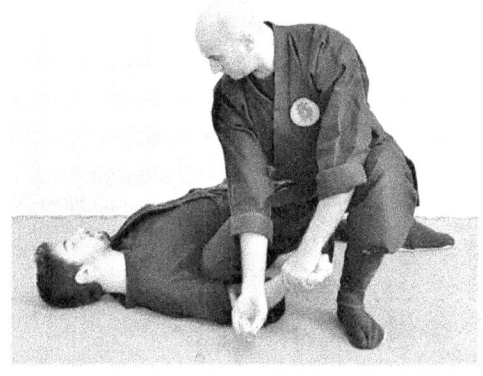

Koshi Ori Itto Dori
腰折り一刀捕り
(Hip break capture of the sword)

The opponent attacks with the Kodachi, from Kata Yaburi no Kamae avoid inside hitting his torso and perform the Koshi Ori technique, disarm and control the opponent.

Kyojitsu

虚実

(True and false, Deception)

Attack with Migi Katate Uchi (this is "Kyo" 虚 false), the opponent blocks your wrist with his left hand, rotate your arm clockwise and grabbing the end of the stick with your left hand perform a Gyaku on the wrist of the opponent (this is "Jitsu" 実 true).

Dogaeshi
胴返し
(Reverse the trunk)

The opponent grabs the collar with both hands to perform a Seoinage throw, from the posture of Kata Yaburi no Kamae, let the stick with your left hand go, pass the stick in front of the opponent's abdomen and grab it again with your left hand, from this position pull arching the opponent's back lead the opponent to the ground, continue to control with the pressure of the stick on his breastbone, throat or arms.

Kataginu

肩衣

(Sleeveless ceremonial robe for samurai)

The opponent attacks grabbing the collar with both hands, from the position of Kata Yaburi no Kamae, perform a Tsuki at the vital point called Asagasumi with the tip of the left end of the stick, with your left hand grab the opponent's left wrist and perform Tsuke Iri bring him to the ground, and control him.

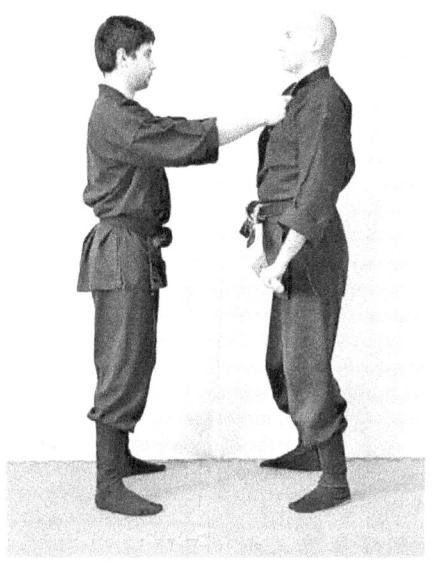

Koku

虚空

(Empty space)

The opponent grabs the right end of the stick with his left hand and grabs the stick in the middle of our hands with his right hand, from the posture of Kata Yaburi no Kamae, bend your legs and take a step forward with your right foot to raise the tip of the stick towards him and then rotate it over his right shoulder, unbalancing him and knocking down to the ground, if he continues to hold the grab with his left hand, perform Ura Gyaku, press the left end on his left hand and press it on his throat to contol him.

Kocho Dori
小蝶捕り
(Little butterfly capture)

The opponent attacks with a right fist, from Kata Yaburi no Kamae avoiding inside and hitting upward under his triceps using one hand, then passing the stick under his arm and grabbing the end of the stick to perform Muso Dori pressing with your elbow, as the opponent resists the technique suddenly turn around and hit the opponent's neck with the stick while perfoming Osoto Gake 大外掛け with your right foot, knocking him down to the ground, keep the stick on his neck from this position and grab his right sleeve while holding the stick with your left hand to block his movements.

Ryufu

龍風

(Wind Dragon)

From Kata Yaburi no Kamae hit the opponent's left arm with Hidari Katate Uchi, taking advantage of the opponent's reaction, when he brings his right hand on his left arm, with your right hand grab his wrist while leaning the stick on your right shoulder, making a step with your left foot in front of the opponent's right foot and put his elbow in the lever by turning your spine, control him by keeping the lever on his arm.

Kote (Torashu)
虎手
(Tiger's claw)

The opponent attacks with a right fist, from Kata Yaburi no Kamae avoid inside and make a thrust to his right shoulder with the left end of the stick in the Kyusho called Jujiro 十字路, hit the opponent's left hand with the right end and then suddenly under his left jaw (Hidari Ago 左顎) knocking him down on the ground, control him Zanshin.

Taki Koi
瀧鯉
(Waterfall carp)

From Kata Yaburi no Kamae hit the Asagasumi vital point with Hane Age Uchi, from this position make a thrust with the tip of the stick in the throat bringing the opponent to the ground (this action is called Tsuki Taosu 突き倒す), control with the stick by pressing in the vital point Jinchu 人中 or in the mouth Ate Osae Dori 当て押え捕り (take great care while training this technique can break or dislocate the jaw).

Chinsoku
沈足
(Submerged leg)

The opponent kicks with his right foot, from Kata Yaburi no Kamae avoid to outside, hitting and sweeping (Uchi Harai 打ち払い) at the opponent's vital point Yaku 扼 with the stick's right end, do a thrust at the vital point Koe 声, and finally capture the leg with the stick and perform a joint-lock to break the leg, for example Ashi Oni Kudaki.

Taki Nagare
瀧流
(Waterfall flow)

The opponent attacks with a right fist, from Kata Yaburi no Kamae avoid outside and hit inside the opponent's right ankle with the right end of the stick, kneel on the left leg putting the foot to the opponent's right foot side, turn the stick and push with the right end of the stick on the armpit to knock down the opponent, he fall on his face, and control him by pressing the stick on his leg and arm Gaisai To Jakkin Itami Osae 外谷と弱筋痛み押え.

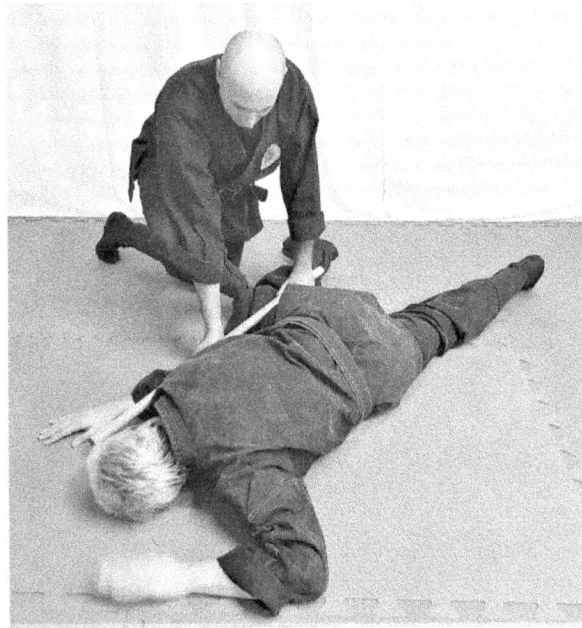

Odori Taoshi Ichi
踊倒し一
(Dance and overthrow, one)

The opponent attacks with a right fist, from Kata Yaburi no Kamae avoid to the right while hitting with the stick's left end below the opponent's right elbow, deflecting his fist, following the action turn the arm clockwise Osu Gotoku Sabaki 押す如く捌き, turn sideways remaining parallel to the opponent, hit with the left end of the stick under his nose, by crunching under his nose through the stick with the arm, Jinchu Gaeshi Uchi Shimeru 人中返し打ち締める, from this position control his right arm and kneel on your left knee on the opponent's right leg to fall down him to the ground.

Odori Taoshi Ni
踊倒し二
(Dance and overthrow, two)

The opponent attacks with a right front kick, from Kata Yaburi no Kamae avoid outside putting the right end under the the opponent's right ankle, from this position perform Sankaku Jime to his ankle with the stick, changing the grip of your right hand turning the stick to rotate the foot, so that the opponent turns his back, and pull to bring him to the ground, control him twisting the ankle while maintaining the painful grip.

Jujisha Ichi
十字車一
(Cross wheel, one)

The opponent attacks with a right fist, from Kata Yaburi no Kamae perform Naname Ushiro Ura Waki Uchi, bring the stick under his right elbow to perform Juji Dori and throw the opponent by placing the left leg in front of the opponent's right leg and turning spine.

Jujisha Ni

十字車二

(Cross wheel, two)

The opponent attacks with a right fist, from Kata Yaburi no Kamae perform Sabaki Dori grabbing with your right hand, bring the left end of the stick behind the opponent's right ankle, while taking a step to the left unbalancing the opponent backwards, from this position grab the end of the stick with your left hand doing a Kotsu Itami Dori 骨痛み捕り (painful bone capture) to the ankle, push with the left elbow on the leg to drop the opponent to the ground on his back, control him, if he will move, hit at any vital point.

Rokai
老怪
(Mysterious elder)

The opponent grabs the collar and sleeve from Kumite 組み手 (Japanese term that derives from the ancient Sumo), he tries a Seoinage throw, from Munen Muso no Kamae stop the throw by lowering your hips, grab the stick passing it in front of his ribs grabbing the other end to do a Do Jime, to his floating ribs (be careful not to break the ribs), you can perform several controls, for example by doing a Shime hitting the Kinteki point by pulling upward, Ashikubi Sankaku Jime and Ashi Onikudaki.

Ten Taoshi
天倒し
(Heaven overthrow)

The opponent attacks with a right fist, from Munen Muso no Kamae hit with Bofuri 棒振り which is Kyo 虚 (false, so it's a feint), do a frontal kick to his face, as your foot comes down grab the stick with both hands and hit at his vital point Tento with the edge of the stick Tokikaku Uchi, knocking the opponent down kneel and control with Naisai Itami Osae Ashi Ori.

Kyoku Shime
曲締め
(Strangulation melody)

The opponent armed with the long sword from Daijodan no Kamae 大上段の構え performs a vertical cut, from Munen Muno no Kamae avoid to inside and hit from below to opponent's left wrist with Katate Furi, with your left hand grab the right wrist of the opponent and his sword, and hit with the tip of the stick Tokikaku Uchi, under his right cheekbone, perform a Shime pressing with the forearm under his throat and the stick behind the neck, kick down the opponent's arm with your left leg to control the sword.

Otonashi
音無し
(Without sound)

The opponent armed with the long sword from Daijodan no Kamae performs a vertical cut, from Otonashi no Kamae without letting read your intentions, quickly kneel on the left leg (Moguri Taihen 潜り体変 diving body movement) and perform a thrust, from here there are endless ways to overthrow your opponent in to the ground.

十方折衝の術

JUPPO SESSHO NO JUTSU
(The art of negotiation in the 10 directions)

The bases of Budo are found in Juppo Sessho no Jutsu, which is also known as Koteki Ryoda Juppo Sessho no Justu 虎擲龍拏十方折衝の術, which is found in the very ancient secret scrolls of Hibun Jujiron Shinden Jukai 祕文十字論師伝寿海, which is part of the Amatsu Tatara scrolls, and they deal with how to fight with short weapons such as Kodachi, Jutte and Tessen against an opponent armed with a long sword because in fact from these techniques were born the techniques known as Muto Dori 無刀捕, that are considered the highest level techniques for a martial artist. The name Koteki Ryoda refers to the legend of a fierce fight between a Tiger and a Dragon and teaches the mental preparation to defend yourself with bare hands in front of an enemy armed with a sword, making the enemy powerless, using the vision of the Tiger and the Dragon. Juppo Sessho no Jutsu 十方折衝の術 (can also be written with the ideograms for "taking life"; Sessho no Jutsu 殺生の術) and is connected to the secrets of Kodachi, Jutte and Tessen, but it is not limited only to these weapons but can be used for any short weapon such as the Hanbo, in fact Juppo Sessho 十方折衝 also has the meaning that "all things are connected", this depends on from your own Sainou 才能 talent, Tamashii 魂 spirit and Utsuwa 器 ability. In order to disarm an opponent with a long or short sword, you must use the Juji Ryoku 十字力, or the power of the correct angle, it is like trapping a bee in the palm of your hand without it stinging you "Amo Isshun no Tamamushi!" 中一瞬の吉丁虫. Following this will be shown the techniques of the Juppo Sessho applied to the techniques of Hanbojutsu, to be able to fully understand this concept it must be learned through Isshin Denshin 以心伝心 communion of heart with heart with the teacher.

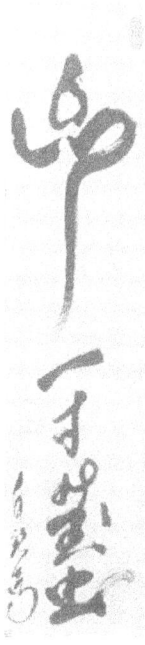

Shodo calligraphic art of "Amo Isshun no Tamamushi" 中一瞬の吉丁虫 painted by Soke Masaaki Hatsumi donated to Shihan Luca Lanaro.

Kiri no Hito Ha (Kata Hane)
桐の一葉(片羽)

(A flower of Paulownia [A wing])

The opponent with the short sword attacks with a thrust, from Kata Yaburi no Kamae avoid outside and let the stick go with your left hand, hit the Kote, from this position advance with the right foot, and hit the opponent's face with the stick, controlling his arm that hold the short sword with your elbow, from here you can make infinite variations Banpen Henka 万変変化.

Rakka (Hane Otoshi)
落花(跳ね落とし)
(Falling petals [Jump and overthrow])

The opponent armed with the long sword from Daijodan no Kamae attacks with a vertical cut, from Otonashi no Kamae avoid jumping outside, by executing Kuri Gaeshi hitting the opponent's right arm to disarm him, perform a Do Jime with the stick by pressing on the breastbone.

Mizu Tori
水鳥
(Water bird)

The opponent with the short sword attacks with a vertical cut, from Kata Yaburi no Kamae kneel and perform a thrust (Moguri Gata 潜型 diving form), "like an aquatic bird that plunges into the water."

Gorin Kudaki (Kote Suso Harai)
五輪碎 (小手裾拂)

("5 elements" smash [Sweep the wrist and the leg])

The opponent with the long sword from Daijodan no Kamae attacks with a vertical cut, from Kata Yaburi no Kamae avoid the attack inside and hit the opponent's left Kote with the stick's left end from top to bottom, you kneel on your left knee and turn the stick clockwise performing Han Gaeshi Uchi hitting his left leg Sune Uchi, knock down the opponent, control Zanshin 残心.

Mawari Dori
廻捕り
(Rotate and capture)

The opponent with the short sword attacks with a thrust, from Kata Yaburi no Kamae avoid outside, hit his wrist with Han Gaeshi Uchi and perform with the stick a Sankaku Jime to the opponent's throat, and bring him to the ground making him hit with his back on your knee (be very careful when performing this control because it is very dangerous).

KI NAGASHI
(Energy flow)

The opponent stands with the Katana in Daijodan no Kamae at your back, he attacks with a vertical cut, from Munen Muso no Kamae feeling the Sakki 殺気 (the intent to kill) of the opponent avoid executing Tate Nagare, kick with your right foot to his Kote and hit with the stick to the opponent's right shin. To perform this technique it is essential to have passed the Sakki Test (an exam performed to pass the 5th Dan in the Bujinkan Dojo).

棒投げ

BO NAGE
(Stick throw)

From Yoko Ichimonji no Kamae let the grip with your left hand go and turn the stick forward with the right hand to throw it against the opponent, like to throw a Shuriken, throw it forward using a whip movement of the wrist horizontally. This is the basic technique, the technique in the following photos instead is the "free throw" Jiyu Nage 自由投げ this strike is also called Sanbou Shinsho 参棒心勝 also written 参謀心勝, changing the ideogram for stick Bou 棒 with the ideogram Bou 謀 strategy, you get "The soldier's winning mentality".

半棒術 伝唱

HANBOJUTSU DENSHO
(Tradition of short stick art)

The Hanbojutsu techniques shown in this chapter are the techniques transmitted as part of the School Kukishin Ryu Happo Bikenjutsu 九鬼神流八法秘剣術. The forms of this school are divided as usually done in the traditional Ryu-Ha 流派, that is divided into three levels: in the Shoden no Kata 初伝の型 "Initial transmission form" we practice short stick combat against the "short sword" Shoto 小刀 , in the Chuden no Kata 中伝の型 "Medium transmission form" we practice short stick combat against the opponent who attacks with bare hands, in the Okuden no Kata 奥伝の型 "the secret transmission form" we practice short stick combat against the "long sword" Daito 大刀.

Hisshi

"Takamatsu Sensei often told me, "Both Toda Sensei and Ishitani Sensei told me that there are rules for the passage of the writings to the disciples. One of these rules is that it is not good to pass on the written transmission (Densho 伝唱). This is due to the fact that the depth of the truth of the martial way is infinite, even if someone reads something written in the Densho or other things that are written about the Budo, simply you study the written words (Hisshi; 筆詩) these are just dead words (Hisshi; 筆死) if you do not master the Bufu 武風 "Martial wind" (the way of martial arts)."

Masaaki Hatsumi

初伝の型

SHODEN NO KATA
(Initial transmission form)

Katate Ori
片手折
(One arm break)

The opponent with the Shoto in his right hand takes a step with his left foot and grabs the lapel with his left hand, then attacks with a thrust stepping forward with his right foot. From Kata Yaburi no Kamae take a step back with your left foot and hit with the stick under the opponent's left elbow, and then hit his other hand's Kote to disarm him.

Tsuki Otoshi
突き落し
(Push down)

The opponent with the Shoto in his right hand takes a step with his left foot and grabs the lapel with his left hand, then attacks with a thrust stepping forward with his right foot. From Kata Yaburi no Kamae take a step back with your left foot and hit with the stick under the opponent's left elbow, you do a thrust stepping forward with your right foot and hit his throat pushing him down (Tsuki Otosu 突き落とす), to overthrow him on the ground.

Uchi Waza
打技
(Strike technique)

The opponent with the Shoto in his right hand attacks with a thrust stepping forward with his right foot. From Kata Yaburi no Kamae take a step back with your left foot to 45 degree and turn the stick in the right hand letting the grip with your left hand and grabbing the end again (Han Gaeshi Uchi), hit with the stick to the right Kote of the opponent to disarm him, hit to his Hidari Kasumi with the Han Gaeshi Uchi movement.

Nagare Dori
流捕
(Flow capture)

The opponent with the Shoto in his right hand attacks with a thrust stepping forward with his right foot. From Kata Yaburi no Kamae avoid inside and letting the stick with your left hand go holding in vertical the stick while grabbing the opponent's wrist, turn the stick and twist his wrist and perform Koshi Ori by rotating the body counterclockwise to bring him on the ground, control him.

Kasumi Gake
霞掛
(In the midst of the mist)

The opponent with the Shoto in his right hand attacks with a thrust stepping forward with his right foot. From Kata Yaburi no Kamae avoid outside and letting the stick with your right hand strike with the stick on the opponent's arm or his torso, by grabbing his right wrist, turning the stick and twisting his wrist perform Tsuke Iri to bring him to the ground, control him.

Yuki Chigai
行違

(To cross without meeting)

The opponent with the Shoto in his right hand attacks with a thrust stepping forward with his right foot. From Kata Yaburi no Kamae avoid outside and let the stick go with your right hand, strike with the stick into the opponent's face grabbing his right wrist. Raise your arm and pass under it to throw the opponent with the technique Katate Nage.

Ate Kaeshi

当返

(To turn upside down and hit)

The opponent with the Shoto in his right hand cuts from top to bottom. From Kata Yaburi no Kamae kneel (Moguri Gata) changing the grip turn upside down the stick with your right hand and do a thrust, striking where you want to the ribs or eyes, face, abdomen or groin.

Kao Kudaki
顔砕
(Face smash)

The opponent with the Shoto in his right hand attacks with a thrust stepping forward with his right foot. From Kata Yaburi no Kamae avoid outside changing the grip rotating the stick in your right hand (Han Gaeshi Uchi), to hit the opponent's Kote or Shoto to disarm him, then hit the Yoko Men by turning the stick with your right hand (similar movement to Hachiji Furi).

中伝の型

CHUDEN NO KATA
(Medium transmission form)

Ipponme
一本目
(First technique)

The opponent grabs the collar with his right hand, from Munen Muso no Kamae pass the tip of the stick under the opponent's arm, and grabbing it from below with your left hand crossing your arms perform Sankaku Jime on his wrist, kneeling on your left leg bring the opponent to the ground.

Nihonme
二本目
(Second technique)

The opponent grabs the lapel with both hands, from Munen Muso no Kamae pass the tip of the stick under his arms and grabbing it from below with your left hand crossing his arms perform Sankaku Jime on his wrists, kneeling on your left leg bring the opponent to the ground.

Sanbonme
三本目
(Third technique)

The opponent grabs the collar with both hands, from Munen Muso no Kamae pass the tip of the stick under the opponent's right arm and grabbing it from underneath crossing the arms with your left hand perform Sankaku Jime at his Kote, freeing yourself from the grab to the lapel, release the grip with your right hand, and by changing the grip hit his left Kote with the stick, and then kick with your right foot to knock down the opponent.

Shihonme
四本目
(Fourth technique)

The opponent grabs your right wrist with his left hand, from Munen Muso no Kamae lower the body and pass the end of the stick under the opponent's wrist, grabbing it from below with your left hand to put a Gyaku, free yourself from his grab, let the stick with your left hand go and hit with Katate Furi to his trunk, if necessary rotate and hit him one more time from the top performing Uchi Otoshi 打ち落とし.

Gohonme
五本目
(Fifth technique)

The opponent grabs your right wrist with both hands, from Munen Muso no Kamae, kneel on your left leg grabbing the stick with the left hand in the lower end, stand up rotating clockwise the top tip unbalancing the opponent to free yourself from his grab, hit from top to bottom, the opponent protects his head by crossing his arms (Jumonji 十文字), immediately make a thrust.

Ropponme
六本目
(Sixth technique)

The opponent attacks with a right fist, from Munen Muso no Kamae execute a Nagashi Uke with your left hand, pass the stick under the opponent's right triceps grabbing it with your left hand, press with your left elbow on his forearm, putting the opponent's arm in the lever, pull to bring the opponent to the ground by kneeling on the right leg, and then do a thrust to the opponent's right side with the stick.

Variation: perform Onikudaki.

Nanahonme
七本目
(Seventh technique)

The opponent grabs your collar and sleeve and attacks with a throw, from Munen Muso no Kamae open the arms and lower the hips in Hira Ichimonji no Kamae of Taijutsu (unarmed fighting) to stop the throw, then with the stick perform a Dojime pressing on his ribs, sweep his legs throwing the opponent to the ground, take a step back and perform a thrust.

Happonme
八本目
(Eighth technique)

The opponent grabs from behind, from Munen Muso no Kamae lower your hips and pass the stick under the opponent's right ankle and pull the stick with both hands and sit on his leg to make him fall backwards, by sitting on his leg to do a lever, turn around opening his legs and press with both knees in the inner thigh of the opponent's legs, if the opponent moves, do a thrust into a vital point.

Kyuhonme
九本目
(Ninth technique)

The opponent grabs the upper end of the stick with his left hand, from Munen Muso no Kamae bring the left hand to the stick and firmly put a joint-lock like Omote Gyaku, Ura Gyaku, Hon Gyaku, any of these is fine. Once the Gyaku is applied, move inside with the body and throw the opponent, rotate the stick and strike him.

Variation: Omote Gyaku.

Yonnin Dori

四人捕

(Four men capture)

Four opponents grabs us, one hugs us from behind, two with both hands grabbing one arm per opponent, and the front opponent grabs the collar with both hands. From Munen Muso no Kamae, swing your body to the right, pass the stick under the right opponent's arms, than place the stick over the person's arms in front of you, then swing the body to throw the opponents, hit the fourth behind you with a thrust, Zanshin.

Sannin Kedori
三人蹴捕
(Three men kicks capture)

Three opponents kicks with the right foot, from Munen Muso no Kamae, with a superior body movement hit the first opponent's kick with Ate Gaeshi, turn the stick and hit the second opponent's leg with Katate Furi, and then capture the kick of the last opponent with the movement of the body and perform a Shimeru on it, from this position hit him with Kinteki Uchi, and finish him with Yoko Men Uchi.

奥伝の型
OKUDEN NO KATA
(The secret transmission form)

Tachi Gonin Dori
太刀五人捕
(Five men with a long sword capture)

Five opponents armed with long swords attack with a vertical cut, from Otonashi no Kamae, avoid the blades of the opponents, moving the body and legs avoid the weapons of the opponents, using the stick hit in their defenseless points (Suki 透き), to take the strength of theirs combative spirit, in this technique it is essential to use the space Kukan 空間, without showing the weapon, the shape of the stick, or the sound Oto 音, not showing any intent.

仕込み杖

SHIKOMI-ZUE
(Concealed blade stick)

The Shikomi-Zue, is the Japanese concealed blade stick, inside the stick hides a blade, this type of weapon was used above all by the Ninja when they used the disguise techniques Hensojutsu 変装術 to bring a weapon without arousing suspicions so without representing a threat. The techniques of Hanbojutsu and Shikomi-Zue are closely related one should train in the techniques of Hanbojutsu alternating the short stick with the Shikomi-Zue, through this practice you can understand the true form of Hanbojutsu. This section will show the applications Ouyou 応用 of some of the previous techniques using the Shikomi-Zue.

八法秘剣
Happo Biken

"I don't just teach the Taijutsu movement. In the Happo Biken 八法秘剣 ("Eight methods and the secret sword"), one must understand the connection between Taijutsu and any weapon. Everything is the same."

Masaaki Hatsumi

Kata Yaburi no Kamae Yori no Shikomi-Zue
型破の構えよりの仕込み杖

(Striking with the concealed blade stick from the posture Kata Yaburi no Kamae Mugamae 型破の構無構 Posture without posture of breaking the form).

Ichimonji Giri
一文字切り

(Cut in horizontal line)

From Kata Yaburi no Kamae advance with your right foot draw the blade of the Shikomi-Zue and cut horizontally from left to right, practice Jodan 上段 high, Chudan 中段 medium and Gedan 下段 low.

Munen Muso no Kamae Yori no Shikomi-Zue
無念無想の構えよりの仕込み杖
(Hitting with the concealed blade stick from the posture without mind and without thoughts)

Age Giri
上げ切り
(Vertical cut upwards)

From Munen Muso no Kamae, block the tip of the Shikomi-Zue between your toes, suddenly draw the blade out cutting vertically upward.

Otonashi no Kamae Yori no Shikomi-Zue
音無しの構えよりの仕込み杖
(Strike with the concealed blade stick from the posture without sound)

Kage Ichimonji Giri
影一文字切り
(Shadow cut in horizontal line)

From Otonashi no Kamae, step forward with the right foot. Draw the Shikomi-Zue blade from behind the back and cut horizontally from left to right, practice Jodan 上段 high, Chudan 中段 medium and Gedan 下段 low.

Kuri Gaeshi
栗返し

("Reversal chestnut" also called Kachiguri no I 勝栗の意 Idea of dried chestnut)

As in the short stick technique, from Otonashi no Kamae rotate the wrist bringing the end of the stick over the right shoulder and draw the blade to cut to the opponent's Kote.

Oni Kudaki Dori

鬼砕き捕り

(Demon smash capture)

Starting from the short stick technique, once you have performed to the opponent's arm Oni Kudaki joint-lock, draw the Shikomi-Zue blade from underneath and control the opponent by threatening him with the blade on the throat.

Omote Gyaku Yori Oni Kudaki
表逆より鬼砕き
(Demon smash from the external twist)

The opponent grabs the collar of your jacket with his right hand, from Kata Yaburi no Kamae with your left hand control the opponent's hand and hit his ribs with the stick, with your left hand performing the Omote Gyaku joint-lock, pass the stick under opponent's arm hooking his neck in this way you apply the Oni Kudaki joint-lock to the same arm, with the left hand let the grab go to grab the stick and hold his arm in the joint-lock between the stick and your forearm, draw the Shikomi-Zue blade and thrust.

Sankaku Jime

三角締め

(Triangle strangling)

The opponent attacks with a right fist, from Kata Yaburi no Kamae avoid outside and diverting the fist pass the end of the stick on his throat by sliding the stick in your left hand letting the grip of the stick with your right hand go, grab the stick again with your right hand performing a Sankaku Jime to the throat, from this position draw the blade of the Shikomi-Zue.

Tsuke Iri Itto Dori
附入り一刀捕り
(Enter and join capture of the sword)

The opponent with the Katana performs a vertical cut, from Kata Yaburi no Kamae avoid outside and hit the opponent's torso, and insert the stick to perform Tsuke Iri, change the grip of the hands, with your left hand grab the right wrist of the opponent and block the stick with the forearm, from this position draw the blade of the Shikomi-Zue and control the opponent by placing the blade on his throat.

Koshi Ori Itto Dori
腰折り一刀捕り
(Hip break capture of the sword)

The opponent with Katana performs a thrust, from Kata Yaburi no Kamae avoid outside and hit the opponent's torso, and insert the stick to perform Koshi Ori, put the stick vertically so that the gravity draws the blade of the Shikomi-Zue and control the opponent by placing the blade on the wrist's veins.

Shikomi-Zue Bo Nage
仕込み杖棒投げ
(Shikomi-Zue stick throw)

The opponent threatens us with the Katana in Chudan no Kamae 中段の構え keeping us at a distance, from Kata Yaburi no Kamae draw the blade of the Shikomi-Zue assuming Unryu no Kamae 雲龍の構え (the dragon's posture of the clouds) while keeping the stick in Yoko Ichimonji no Kamae, from this posture throw the stick with a sudden movement of the wrist, while the opponent defends himself from the stick, kneel Moguri Gata 潜り型 and cut the opponent's abdomen.

GOSHINJUTSU
(Self-defense)

In self-defense or Goshinjutsu it isn't only important to know how to fight unarmed, but also to know the use of weapons, to learn to use the short stick art is fundamental for various reasons, one is that if you use a gun to defend yourself you will be forced to use it, if you are forced to use it is very easy that you can kill the aggressor, then paying the consequences risking to be accused of excessive self-defense, even using a knife it is very dangerous to control an opponent, while instead with a stick you can keep your opponent at a distance, and you can use it to hit him in the less lethal vital points or use it to put levers and joint-lock without excessively hurting your opponent, also you can use as a weapon any kind of stick like a mop, and walking sticks, umbrellas, etc.

Shizen

"In a real fight you do not have time to remember the techniques, your reaction time would be too slow. Train yourself to not interfere with your natural reactions."

Masaaki Hatsumi

Hanbo Tai Hanbo
半棒対半棒

(Short stick versus short stick)

You often see in stick versus stick fights, that the practitioner blocks high the strike by raising the stick, this is not an effective method, because if it will break you can hurt yourself, also as seen from the photos you can easily be disarmed by a strike at the fingers. Instead of making a block you must receive with the body by sliding the stick being careful to the fingers (this action is called Ukemi 受け身), and from this position you can hit the opponent.

Hanbo Tai Naifu
半棒対ナイフ
(Short stick versus knife)

The opponent attacks grabbing the wrist trying to stab us, using the mop, kick with his left foot the mop to hit the opponent in the groin, the opponent tries a thrust, change the grip to deflect his thrust and turn the knife against him, control him.

The opponent attacks with a thrust, from Munen Muso no Kamae avoid outside and strike at the hands with Katate Furi disarming the opponent, returning to the starting Kamae stepping on the stick to hit the opponent's knee or his foot, (made it dynamicly is easy to break the limb, so in practice, always perform the technique with caution).

Kasa no Goshinjutsu
傘の護身術
(Self-defense with umbrella)

A drunk man approaches the girl with an umbrella and tries to harass her by placing one arm at her side, suddenly the girl hits the face of the assailant with the umbrella handle and closes the umbrella, puts the handle behind the arm to perform the technique Muso Dori and overthrow the opponent to the ground.

警察の逮捕術

KEISATSU NO TAIHOJUTSU
(Police arrest techniques)

Budo Taijutsu is a very old martial art brought to us intact in its effectiveness by Soke Masaaki Hatsumi who is the successor of 9 traditional Japanese martial arts schools developed and practiced by Ninja and Samurai throughout Japanese history, transmitted to him in his full effectiveness by Grandmaster Takamatsu Toshitsugu who worked in China during the Second World War as bodyguard and intelligence (information gathering), using these arts successfully on the field.

The Grand Master Masaaki Hatsumi has influenced with his martial art the training of: SAS, Texas Rangers, FBI, CIA, Marines, Mossad, etc., receiving various awards from various heads of state.

In ancient Japan, the Ninja were also used as police forces, thanks to their ever actual fight techniques, such as the techniques of arrest Taihojutsu 逮捕術, techniques for the use of firearms Teppo no Jutsu 鉄砲術, disarming techniques Muto Dori 無刀捕り, as well as strategies Heihojutsu 兵法術 and techniques of psychological control Shinnenjutsu 心念術 of the adversary and development of self-control with spiritual refinement Seishinteki Kyoho 精神的教養. This section will show some techniques of the short stick used by the police, such as blocking and arresting an attacker with the stick without injuring him.

チームワーク
Teamwork

"When using teamwork technique be aware of the topography and geography of the area. Be aware of the trees, etc. (Forcing your opponent against a tree is one way to prevent escape, for example). This principle applies to conflagration techniques or to people on horses as well."

Masaaki Hatsumi

Tsuke Iri Dori
附入り捕り
(Enter and join capture)

Starting from the basic technique Tsuke Iri previously seen you can practice different variations and controls, in fact it is also used by the Japanese police to control the criminals, below are shown some possible controls starting from this technique.

Once the stick is inserted as for the Tsuke Iri technique, a) blocking his arm with the stick and your left arm, from this position with the other hand you can handcuff or frisk; b) changing the grip by placing a double Ohgyaku in his arms, you can make the opponent walk to take him where you want; c) inserting the stick between the legs you overthrow the opponent to control him on the ground sitting on the stick with Itami Osae on his thigh and biceps, if the opponent attacks with a fist you can easily block it, as well as a kick with his left leg blocking it with your right knee immobilizing the opponent.

Tsuke Iri

a)

b)

c)

Zanshin
残心
(Continued alertness)

The opponent tries to steal the gun from behind, "feeling" the opponent, turn around and imprison his hand with the stick using the Take Ori joint-lock, change the joint-lock applying an Omote Gyaku with the left hand blocking the stick between the opponent's arm and neck, draw the gun with your right hand and control him.

Futari Taihojutsu
二人逮捕術
(Couple arrest technique)

Both practitioners are armed with a short stick to keep the opponent at a distance to try to avoid using force and make him bring back to reason, the opponent suddenly attacks, the attacked agent executes Maki Age and the other Ashi Dori, bringing the criminal to the ground without damaging him, and handcuffing him (this technique can also be performed with policeman's club).

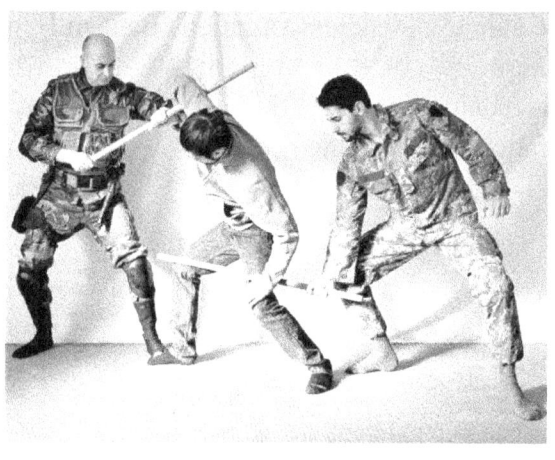
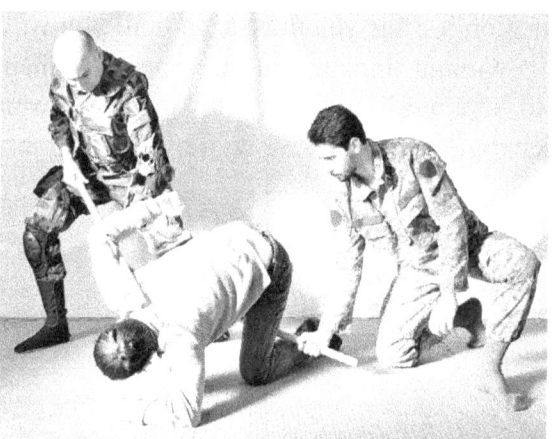
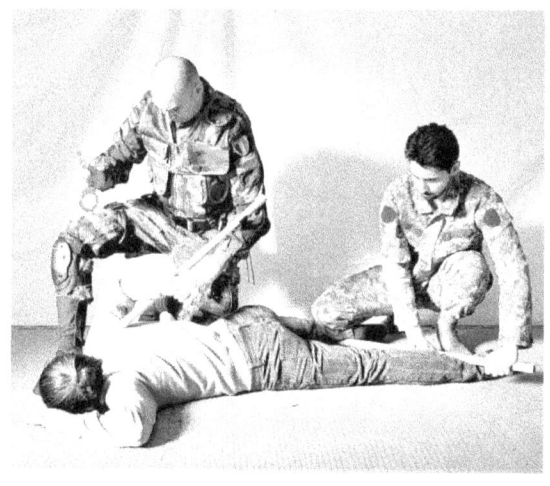
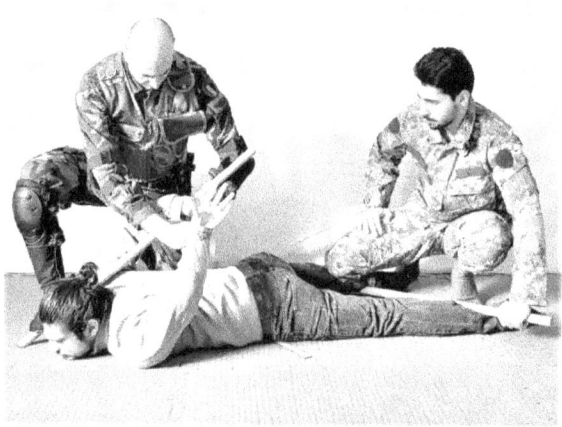

詒変の棒

Ihen no Bo
(Deception of the stick)

A common stick can be used for many things, for example to enter in enemy territory without arousing suspicion, using the stick as a common walking stick. This type of strategies changed according to the situation. This example shows how a slight change in the idea (Ihen 意変) of what really is the art of using even a simple stick can increase your ability in the practice of Hanbojutsu techniques, this concept is known as Ihen no Bo 詒変の棒 and is applied to any kind of stick.

In the art of using the stick no matter what length is, there are techniques called "Kangi" 槓技 or leverage techniques, the basis of these techniques is to be free to respond to the situation, taking advantage of deception Kyojitsu 虚実, for example on the battlefield if you wanted to hit an opponent on horseback, first you hit the horse and then hit the horseman. So your only limit is your imagination for this you must train until you will be able to do endless variations Banpen Henka 万変変化 without thinking, in the state of Munen Muso 無念無想 or Mushin 無心 to do what we need to save our life without thinking about which technique we must do, in fact we are not doing the technique ourself but we do it by "divine" inspiration thanks to the Kami 神.

Glossario

Akuheki 悪癖: bad habit; vice
Amatsu Tatara Hibun 天津蹈鞴秘文: ancient scrolls containing the secrets of Japanese martial arts
Ate 当: hit
Banpenfugyo 万変不驚: 10,000 changes no surprise
Bo 棒: stick, cane, pole (rokushakubo 六尺棒 stick six feet long)
Bokken – Bokuto 木剣: wooden sword
Budo 武道: martial artist
Budoka 武道者: martial artist
Bufu-ikkan 武風一貫: the martial way as a rule, each day of your life, literally, "living through martial wind"
Bujinkan 武神館: residence of the god of war
Bunbu Ryodo 文武両道: (accomplished in) both the literary and military arts
Buyu 武友: martial artist friend
Daisho 大小: large and small; matched pair of long and short swords (symbol of the samurai caste)
Fudoshin 不動心: imperturbable spirit (or immutable)
Ganbatte 頑張って: do your best; go for it; hold on; keep at it
Gokui 極意: deepest level (of an art, skill, etc.); secret teachings; mysteries; innermost secrets
Gorin 五輪: five rings
Goshinjutsu 護身術: art of self-defense
Gyaku 逆: reverse; opposite; joint-lock
Hanbo 半棒: short stick
Happobiken 八法秘剣: eight methods secret sword
Henka 変化: change; variation; alteration; mutation; transition; transformation
Hidari 左: left
Jutsu 術: art; technique
Kaiten 回転: roll; rotation; revolution
Kaizen 改善: improve, taking small steps at the beginning and then increasing
Kakushi Buki 隠し武器: concealed weapons
Kanji 漢字: Chinese characters
Kankaku 感覚: sense; sensation; feeling; intuition
Kata 型: model; type; pattern; standard form of a movement
Katachi 形: shape, form, style
Katana 刀: (single-edged) Japanese sword
Kihon Waza 基本技: basic techniques
Kiso 基礎: foundation; basis
Kocho 小蝶: small butterfly
Kukan 空間: space; airspace
Kyojitsu 虚実: truth and falsehood, feint
Migi 右: right
Nagashi 流し: flow
Nage 投: to throw; to cast away
Maai 間合い: interval; distance; distance between opponents
Rei 礼: thanks; gratitude; manners; etiquette; bow; reward; gift; ceremony; ritual

Ryu 流: fashion; way; style; manner; school
Sabaki 捌き: footwork, shift
Sakkijutsu 殺気術: techniques to perceive the murderous intent
Senpai 先輩: senior (at work or school); superior; elder
Sensei 先生: teacher; master
Shingitai Ichi Jo 心技体一情: the heart, the technique and the body acting as one
Shihan 師範: Title of "Master" is a Japanese Honorific Title, Expert
Shizen 自然: nature; natural, spontaneous
Soke 宗家: the head family. In the realm of Japanese traditional arts, it is used synonymously with the term iemoto. Thus, it is often used to indicate "headmaster"
Taijutsu 体術: classical form of martial art, unarmed fighting
Taisabaki 体捌き: body movement
Tantou 短刀: short sword; dagger
Teashi 手足: hands and feet; limbs
Tengu 天狗: long-nosed goblin (Tengu are a class of supernatural creatures found in Japanese folklore, art, theater, and literature.); braggart
Tsuyoi 強い: strong; powerful; mighty; potent
Ugoki 動き: movement, move, motion; fluctuation
Zanshin 残心: continued alertness; unrelaxed alertness; remaining on one's guard; being prepared for a counterstroke

Japanese numbers
Ichi 一 : one
Ni 二 : two
San 三 : three
Shi (Yon) 四 : four
Go 五 : five
Roku 六 : six
Shichi (Nana) 七 : seven
Hachi 八 : eight
Ku (Kyu) 九 : nine
Ju 十 : ten
Ju ichi 十一 : eleven
Ju ni 十二 : twelve
Ju ku 十九 : nineteen
Ni ju 二十 : twenty
San ju 三十 : thirty
Shi ju 四十 : fourty
Go ju 五十 : fifty
Hyaku 百 : hundred
Sen 千 : thousand
Ban 万 : ten thousand

Bibliography:

Texts of Reference:
Stick Fighting   Masaaki Hatsumi Q. Chambers
Hanbojutsu, Juttejutsu, Tessenjutsu   Masaaki Hatsumi
Ninjutsu, history and tradition   Masaaki Hatsumi
The grandmaster's book of ninja training   Masaaki Hatsumi
Essence of ninjutsu   Masaaki Hatsumi
Understand? Good play!   Masaaki Hatsumi
The way of the Ninja, secret techniques   Masaaki Hatsumi
Advanced stick fighting   Masaaki Hatsumi
Shinden Kihon: Unarmed fighting basic techniques of the Ninja and Samurai   Luca Lanaro

The author:

Shihan 師範 Luca Lanaro, author of the book "Shinden Kihon: Unarmed fighting basic techniques of the Ninja and Samurai", is a regular member of the Shidoshikai (International Bujinkan Instructors Register), and teaches in Genoa from 1999, every year he goes to Japan to study directly with Soke Masaaki Hatsumi, he also gives seminars in Italy and abroad. He was awarded by Soke Masaaki Hatsumi with martial name (Bugou 武号) Isamu Koma 勇駒 which can be translated as "brave horse" (Koma 駒 is the ideogram for chess horse Japanese Shogi, which is a very important piece, while Isamu 勇 means; brave, courageous and heroic), and in February 2017 he received the gold medal of the Bujinkan Dojo.

Website: http://bujin.altervista.org
Facebook: Bujinkan Dojo Genova
YouTube: Bujinkan Dojo Genova
Email: infobujinkan@gmail.com

www.ingramcontent.com/pod-product-compliance
Lightning Source LLC
Chambersburg PA
CBHW082358170426
43191CB00048B/1678